HIRING
FOR
INNOVATION

HIRING
FOR
INNOVATION

Identifying Innovation Skills and Competencies in Job Candidates

DAVID MASUMBA

Printed in the United States of America

ISBN Paperback: 978-1-7341913-0-1
ISBN eBook: 978-1-7341913-1-8

Book Cover and Interior Design: Ghislain Viau

CONTENTS

PREFACE

*"Our heroes are innovators. We stand for innovation.
If you want to work at Apple, we expect you to innovate."*
—Steve Jobs, former Apple CEO

At most of my innovation speaking and training events, I often say that in today's innovation global economy, having an effective system for hiring innovation talent is a vital requirement for advancing workforce innovation across functional units of the organization. In recent years, analysts and commentators on workplace trends have observed that work performance trends are shifting away from "routine work" toward innovation performance, so innovation skills is a top hiring priority across industries. However, desiring to hire workforces with the right innovation skills and abilities is one thing— having the institutional capability to do so is another. This is so because—as it is often said although every person has the inherent capacity to innovate, not everybody possesses the innovation abilities, can-do attitude, self-motivation, or desire to ignite their inherent capacity to actualize it into innovation potential.

This means that if an organization desires to have workforces that will drive innovation performance and contribute to meeting innovation needs in terms of achieving functional unit goals and corporate innovation goals, it's of absolute necessity for the organizational leadership to implement the right tools and approaches for identifying and hiring job candidates with the right innovation skill sets and abilities. However, this cannot be achieved using non-innovation oriented traditional talent recruitment methods and tools.

So this book suggests tools and approaches for identifying and determining the right mix of innovation skill sets for both *experienced* and *entry-level* hires.

Chapter One

INTRODUCTION

Overview

A number of talent-related surveys have revealed that many companies across the globe are facing challenges in finding the right talent. For instance, surveys of employers worldwide conducted by ManpowerGroup, a US-based human resources consulting company, revealed a steady rise in the number of companies experiencing difficulties in finding job candidates with the right skills. In its 2015 survey, ManpowerGroup revealed that more than a third (38 percent) of nearly 40,000 employers worldwide were having difficulties in filling vacancies. In a 2014 global KPMG survey, the majority of respondents (about 59 percent) agreed that there is a new war for talent and that the skill shortages are likely to increase. Similarly, the Chartered Institute of Professional and Development (CIPD)/ Hays 2015 Resourcing and Talent Planning survey in the UK, revealed that skill shortages were escalating. The report showed that over four-fifths (80 percent) of the respondents feel that competition for well-qualified talent had increased over the past two years. The survey report was based on responses from 520 UK-based organizations.

According to a 2016 study by a US-based talent recruitment company Indeed, a talent shortage is hurting innovation across industries. The study revealed that due to that shortage, 80 percent of US-based hiring managers stated that the shortage of skilled manpower was affecting the revenues of their organizations due to a slowdown in market expansion and product development.

It's common knowledge that in today's innovation-driven global economy, in which, for a company to outcompete its competitors, it has to attract and hire diverse innovation talent to meet short- and long-term needs. However, finding job candidates with the right innovation skills is difficult, given that study after study shows that innovation is now the top priority in most industries across the globe. For instance, in Boston Consulting Group's survey of *The 2015 Most Innovative Companies*, 80 percent of respondents indicated innovation as being either a top priority or a top-three priority at their company.

What does this mean? It implies a significant emphasis on the acquisition of innovation talent by hiring managers in many companies. This, therefore, underscores the importance of enacting innovation talent recruitment policies and strategies across industries…hence the need for this book!

In highlighting the shortage of innovation talent, a PwC survey of 2017 revealed that 77 percent of CEOs across the global struggle to find the innovation skills they need. Furthermore, because of the importance of innovation in career development and the shortage of innovation talent, a number of corporations are now using a culture of innovation as a vital tool for enhancing employee engagement. According to a report (*2014 Trends in Global Employee Engagement*), innovation now is a differentiating recruitment and engagement driver for millennials. "Accordingly, innovation is ranked as a top 5 engagement driver for millennials and top-three for generation X and baby boomer workers", stated the report.

Given the emphasis on innovation by corporations and the difficulties corporations are experiencing in identifying innovation talent, this book suggests some tools and approaches for implementing a framework for sourcing diverse innovation talent to meet innovation needs of the organization, i.e. achieving functional unit and corporate innovation goals. Thus, this first chapter focuses on the following four aspects:

1. Reason for this book

2. Interpretation of the phrase *Hiring for Innovation*

3. *Definition of Innovation*

4. Objectives of this book

5. Structure of this book

The details of the above aspects are as follows:

1. Reason for this book

This book is based on the following four premises:

Lack of tools for identifying innovation talent

One of the common questions I get at most of the innovation training events that I conduct is, "What tools can one apply to identify and determine innovation skills in job candidates?" Earlier, we noted that a number of studies have observed that many companies now perceive innovation as either a top priority or a top three priority. Further, it's common knowledge that the corporate world perceives innovation as a fundamental strategy in driving corporate growth. Because of this, there is a rush for innovation talent. The question is whether hiring managers have the right tools for identifying that talent? Many experts on talent recruitment have observed that many traditional corporate recruiting processes cannot be applied to hire candidates with desired innovation skills. For instance, at the *20*th *Annual International Conference on Development and Open Innovation*, held from February 11–13, 2013 in La Jolla, California, one of the keynote speakers—Dr. John Sullivan, a renowned expert on talent management—indicated that talent management has a unique opportunity to play a major role in corporate innovation. However, Dr. Sullivan observed that many managers lack the right talent management skills required to drive innovation management. "Unfortunately," he noted, "many current talent management and HR processes were designed in the 20th century not with the focus on innovation but instead with an emphasis on administration, reducing costs and legal issues. Take the recruiting process for example; the normal talent recruiting process that is designed to hire a large volume of typical workers simply won't be effective in attracting innovators,"

And at a conference on innovation held at Harvard Business School in 2007, panelists felt that traditional management practices have little to contribute to the innovation performance of an organization. Many panelists felt that the current traditional models were stacked against innovation performance. In other words, if innovation is to thrive in organizations, functional units will have to align innovation performance to their respective practices and systems.

In the context of talent recruitment practices, what does the above statement imply? One of the implications is that it is difficult for corporations to identify job applicants with the required levels and mixtures of innovation skills and abilities using conventional methods of talent recruitment. The question is: what talent recruitment methods and techniques can you apply to identify job applicants with particular innovation skills that the organization is looking for? The intention of this book is to suggest tools for identifying, assessing, and determining the right innovation skills and other innovation attributes in job candidates for both experienced and entry-level hires.

Companies experience difficulties in identifying innovation talent

Earlier, we stated that a number of studies have revealed that companies across the globe are facing challenges in finding the right talent; and this is, to some extent, hurting innovation, which in turn is slowing down market expansion and product development. The question here is could it be that what is hurting innovation in many companies, besides the general shortage of talent, is the difficulty, specifically in identifying talent, with the right innovation skills in the job market? Remember, earlier, we referred to a 2017 survey of CEOs across the globe in which 77 percent of the CEOs struggle to find job candidates with the right innovation skills. Because of the difficulties in finding talent with innovation skills in the job market, a number of companies are designing initiatives aimed at attracting talent with innovation potential at universities. For instance, an annual report by a US-based institute—The Institute for Corporate Productivity—released in April 2013, revealed that most companies are now finding talent with innovative potential in colleges even before graduation, citing companies such as Qualcomm, a US-based technology company. So, the intention of this book is to provide skills and tools for identifying talent with innovation skills and contribute to easing the difficulties companies face in hiring talent with the right mix of innovation skill sets.

Innovation talent recruitment practices is an essential element for building cross-functional innovation capabilities

In organization context, capabilities are generally interpreted as an interconnected set of systems, tools, processes, skills and knowledge that a company builds over a given period to drive sustainable growth and competitiveness. So, in terms of innovation, one would describe innovation capabilities as: *an interconnected set of innovation systems, innovation-related tools, innovation-related processes, and innovation skills and knowledge that an organization builds to contribute to advancing a culture of innovation across functional units, which ultimately contribute to driving corporate growth and competitiveness.*

So, how does this relate to hiring for innovation? The relationship is that hiring for innovation practices are part of the interconnected system of capabilities responsible for supplying innovation talent that is vital to advancing and sustaining corporate-wide innovation performance. This means that innovation talent recruitment practices are an essential component for building corporate innovation capabilities and, as stated earlier, a vital capability for advancing corporate-wide innovation performance. Because of the critical role that innovation talent plays in advancing innovation across functional units, a number of experts in the field of innovation have often emphasized the need for organizations to enact recruitment strategies for hiring innovation talent if organizations are to advance innovation performance across functional units. For instance, in an article, Michael Stanleigh—CEO of Business Improvement Architects, a US-based business consulting firm—observed that creating a culture of innovation starts with the hiring approaches. "Hiring for innovation", Stanleigh notes, "presents new challenges to traditional hiring practices and requires nothing less than an innovative approach."

As a way of advancing innovation practices, CEOs in some of the most innovative companies emphasize—and also ensure—that new hires have the ability to contribute to innovation. For instance, in an interview with the media sometime in 2012, Amazon CEO Jeff Bezos described the role he plays in identifying job candidates with innovation skills. Bezos ensures that every manager at Amazon possesses innovative thinking abilities, and he routinely checks innovation goals for his managers. It is also reported that Bezos poses one common question to new hires, especially managers. He asks them whether they have ever invented or innovated anything. At Virgin, CEO Richard Branson has made innovation one of six key aspects the company assesses when screening job applicants. "To get hired at Virgin", according to one report, "you must demonstrate a passion for new ideas, you must make your creativity apparent, and show a track record of thinking differently."

Google is also another company that uses an innovative technique for finding innovative job candidates called Google Code Jam, a problem-solving tournament where participants compete online to solve the same problems under the same time constraints. The prize for winning is $10,000 and a job offer from Google. Through use of the tournament, Google effectively screens 21,000 worldwide applicants for jobs in a matter of days with a format that is almost entirely automated. While the early qualifying rounds largely test an individual's speed in solving computer programming problems, the final challenge phase, conducted with the hundred finalists at Google's headquarters, asks the participant to demonstrate more innovative thinking; each contestant attempts to crack the programming code of the other participants. This process has been very successful at helping Google find highly talented and creative programmers. And Steve Jobs, the late former Apple CEO, is quoted to have often said, "Our heroes are innovators. We stand for innovation. If you want to work at Apple, we expect you to innovate."

Organizations are now seeking to broaden innovation capabilities across functional units

According to studies and experts on innovation, the perception of innovation in the corporate world has changed. In that, the conventional approach to innovation in organizations has been that innovation is a responsibility of specific functional units and professionals. But many organizations have now realized the disadvantage in this approach. Relying on one functional unit and a few individuals exposes an organization to the risk of not matching up to the organization's demands for innovation. For this reason, many organizations are now seeking to broaden innovation capabilities across functional units. According to a 2010 Institute for Corporate Productivity study on the topic of innovation, virtually all 641 respondents representing organizations with 1,000 or more employees agreed that innovation increased in importance across their organizations, and it further predicted that innovation will become more important in the next five years. How does broadening innovation performance across functional units relate to innovation talent recruitment practices? Because recruitment practices are the instruments and avenues used to identify and supply talent in driving the organization mission and also meeting corporate growth objectives, it is essential that an organization aligns or systemizes innovation performance to its talent recruitment practices, and use the innovation talent practices to hire job applicants with talent or with potential attributes to contribute to advancing innovation in the organization.

An effective tool for attracting and retaining high-performing talent

Some studies have observed that using innovation as a factor for recruitment is a magnet for attracting and retaining top talent. A 2014 Hay Group report predicted that through 2018, the global labor markets will see unprecedented talent movement, with 24 percent of the global workforce changing jobs, and that to succeed in today's and the next few years' job market, innovation is one of the key recruiting tools. According to Deloitte's 2014 study *"The Millennials,"*, millennials will comprise 75 percent of the global workforce by 2025, and that innovation improves the recruiting "career perception" of the organization. "This is especially true, for millennials who want to work for organizations that foster innovative thinking, develop their skills, and make a positive contribution to society,", reads the report.

2. Interpretation of the Phrase *"Hiring for Innovation"*

This is a process that involves two main aspects. First, implementation of tools and skill development programs for adopting innovation talent recruitment practices. The second aspect involves the application of the tools and the process to identify the right innovation skill sets in job candidates for both experienced and entry-level job positions across functional units of an organization.

3. Definition of Innovation

In chapter two, step 4, we have given a detailed definition of innovation, and why it is important to understand the meaning of innovation when undertaking innovation talent recruitment practices. In a nutshell, innovation is a process that involves identifying a problem, then generating an innovative idea—never seen on the market before to fix the problem—and transforming the innovative idea into a solution, then converting the innovative solution into monetary value.

4. Objectives of this Book

To educate the audience:

- That one of the critical aspects to undertake is hiring for innovation.

- That you cannot use non-innovation oriented traditional recruitment methods to identify and hire innovation talent.

- How to apply innovation-oriented tools to identify different types of innovation skill sets and competencies in job candidates.

- How to apply different innovation-oriented tools to identify innovation talent in experienced hires and entry-level job candidates.

5. Structure of this Book

The book is structured in thirteen steps in five chapters for designing and implementing a mechanism or framework of tools for identifying innovation skills in job candidates.

Chapter Two
PRELIMINARY ASPECTS

There are six steps in this chapter:

- Step 1: Conducting a situation analysis
- Step 2: Describing the organization vision
- Step 3: Outlining the core and support functional units
- Step 4: Understanding the meaning of innovation
- Step 5: Understanding innovation dimensions
- Step 6: Aligning the meaning of innovation to functional units and business segments

Step 1: Situation Analysis

Conducting situation analysis is the first step for creating a framework for identifying and hiring job candidates with the right innovation skill sets. The process involves determining whether the organization's existing talent recruitment framework or practices have elements about identifying innovation skills in job candidates for both experienced and entry-level hires.

To understand *situation analysis* in the context of innovation talent recruitment, the first step includes: (1) definition of situation analysis in the context of innovation talent recruitment practices, (2) why it's important to conduct situation analysis, and (3) an example of a table for conducting a simple situation analysis when implementing mechanism for hiring for innovation across functional units.

Definition of situation analysis

We define situation analysis in the context of hiring for innovation as follows: *a process that involves assessing the organization's existing talent recruitment practices to determine the extent to which innovation competencies are included.*

Importance

Situation analysis provides data that informs the leadership of what aspects should be included in the innovation talent recruitment framework or framework hiring for innovation, and to what extent certain innovation talent recruitment tools and techniques should be adopted.

Example

Here is an example of a table for conducting a simple situation analysis when creating an innovation talent recruitment framework.

Table 2:1. Situation analysis

Example of a table for conducting situation analysis	
Elements of the organization's talent recruitment practices: *What are the main and vital process aspects of the organization's talent recruitment practices?*	Has the organization aligned innovation performance to the talent recruitment practices stated in this table? If so, outline how:
1.	
2.	
3.	
4.	
5.	
6.	
7.	
Conducted by:	
Date situation analysis was conducted:	

The CEO must support the exercise

For any major innovation support initiative to succeed, CEO support is critical. Adopting an innovation talent recruitment framework is a major innovation-support undertaking that requires unwavering support of the CEO and top leadership of the organization. So, ensure that the idea of introducing an innovation talent recruitment framework is well supported by the top leadership, including the CEO, because without gaining sufficient mindshare and support of the CEO, it will be a huge uphill exercise that will result in a flop.

A number of experts on innovation have observed that it is almost impossible to systemize innovation across an organization without the support of the CEO. For instance, when asked about the role of the CEO in advancing and sustaining innovation across the organization, Chairman and CEO for Procter & Gamble A. G. Lafley responded in an interview with the Harvard Business Review on March 8, 2008 that no innovation thrives in an organization without support of the CEO. Lafley is credited for his "leadership for innovation strategy" which he initiated after taking over as President and CEO in 2002, creating a collaborative culture in which "innovation was everybody's job" at P&G.

In a 2007 survey of 601 senior executives by Accenture called *Overcoming Barriers to Innovation*, one of the key findings was that the role of the CEO in driving innovation performance in an organization was critical. In short, the role and support of the top leadership in the organization, beginning with the CEO, in advancing and sustaining a culture of innovation across the organization is a key requirement for implementation and eventual success of any innovation practice. According to a report by the Innovation Resource—an innovation consulting company based in Santa Barbara, CA—the single most important trait of those who sustained growth through innovation were those companies with ongoing CEO involvement. Among them, according to the report were IBM, Whirlpool, Procter & Gamble, Borg-Warner, and GE. According to the report, though these companies appointed a senior person to be in charge of institutionalizing and systemizing innovation, their CEOs never abdicated responsibility entirely.

The bottom line is that the CEO should be involved in establishing various committees that will be responsible for overseeing the process of designing and implementing innovation talent recruitment practices, beginning with the committee that will be established to conduct situation analysis for determining the extent to which the organization has aligned innovation performance to the organization's talent recruitment practices.

Step 2: Describe the Organizational Vision

This section involves describing the relationship between organization vision and innovation talent recruitment. The aspects include: (1) the definition of innovation vision, (2) perspectives of organization vision (3) why it's important to understand the organization vision when designing and applying the innovation talent recruitment tools.

Definition of Organizational Vision

What is an organizational vision? Organizations use different phrases to define their vision. For the purposes of this book, a company vision is a picture expressed in the form of a statement of what the organization would like to be in a defined time period. The latter part of the definition is what distinguishes a *vision* from a *strategy*, an aspect that is often misunderstood in many organizations. A vision is normally what the organization would like to be in, for instance, the next three to five years; the strategy is how the company is going to realize that vision.

Perspectives of organizational vision

In many cases, companies have different perspectives on how to formulate their visions. Some companies have a one sentence vision statement; others take a multidimensional approach in which the organizational vision is expressed from more than one perspective, such as two, three, or four vision perspectives focusing on core concepts. For example, one company's organizational vision might consist of the following four vision perspectives:

- *Market share vision perspective,* which takes into account what the company intends to be like in relation to market share within a defined timeframe.

- *Market leadership vision perspective*, which outlines the company's vision to be a market leader over a specified time frame.

- *Revenue vision perspective*, outlines the financial vision of the company over a specified period. In other words, how much revenue does the company intend to generate in the next three to five years?

- *Shareholder value vision perspective*, which outlines the desired percentage of growth in dividends over a specified period.

Bottom line: Whatever style or approach the organization adopts to formulate the organizational vision, it must be simple, clear, and should be understood by everyone in the organization.

Importance

Why is it important to understand the relationship between organization vision and hiring for innovation? For two reasons:

i. Job applicants should be made to understand how vital innovation is to the realization of the organization vision. Earlier, we described four aspects on which this book is premised, one of which is that the perception of corporate innovation is changing. Many organizations, according to a number of studies, are now seeking to broaden innovation performance capabilities across functional units, unlike in the past, when innovation was generally viewed as a responsibility of specific functional units and professionals. We also stated that because recruitment practices are the instruments and avenues used to identify and supply talent for driving the organization mission—and also meeting corporate growth objectives—it is vital that an organization aligns or systemizes innovation performance to its talent recruitment practices while using the innovation talent practices to contribute toward instilling in the hearts and minds of its workforces—also to inform job applicants that innovation performance is everyone's business, from the newest recruit. So, job applicants must understand, from their first contact with the organization, what its vision is and how vital innovation is to realizing it.

ii. It enables the leadership to understand the right mixture of innovation talent the organization needs to contribute toward realizing the organization vision. Studies have observed that in a number of cases, differences between less and more successful corporations in terms of growth is innovation. For instance, in its April 2013 study, the US-based Institute for Corporate Productivity revealed that high-performing corporations are three times more likely to implement practices that drive innovation. What is the relevance of this? That high corporate performance translates into realizing organization vision. That said, it is important for the leadership to understand the connection between innovation talent recruitment and realizing the organization vision. And that in order to achieve functional unit and corporate innovation goals that ultimately contribute toward realizing the organization vision, an organization needs to have the right numbers and types of innovation skill sets across functional units. However, that can only be achieved if the organization has effective innovation talent recruitment tools for sourcing job candidates with the right type of innovation skill sets.

Bottom line: Leadership should therefore ensure that those responsible for designing innovation talent recruitment policies and practices describe (in simple terms) how critical innovation performance is to realizing the organization vision and should also be able to describe the role of the organization's innovation talent recruitment model in contributing to realizing the organization vision. Furthermore, the innovation talent recruitment policies and procedures should clearly describe how the leadership expects everyone in the organization to contribute toward innovation performance. Information about how critical innovation is to vision realization must therefore be well packaged and should be accessible to job applicants from the very first time they make contact with the organization, up to the end of the hiring process, which is usually an induction exercise.

It's important for leadership to not only understand the connection between the organization vision and innovation talent recruitment practices, but also be able to communicate and educate job applicants and new entrants about the organization's innovation talent recruitment practices.

Step 3: Outline the Core and Support Functional Units

What does outlining the core and support functional units entail? Normally, an organization is configured in particular structures, depending on its type of business model and vision. However, in whatever way it is structured, there are two structural categories that every organization consists of: core and support (back-office) functional units. Thus, this section describes core and support functions in relation to innovation talent recruitment practices. This includes: (1) interpretation core and support functional units, (2) importance of outlining core and support functional units, (3) illustration of core and support functional units.

Interpretation of core and support functional units

Core functional units are centered on the organization's main or essential business activities. Usually, core functional units are those that are directly involved in driving the organization's mission. For instance, in a furniture manufacturing company, the design and production functional units would be considered core, whereas finance and accounting units would be support functional units. Also, core units vary from organization to organization, depending on the business model and size.

Support functional units comprise functional activities that are aimed at supporting achievement of strategic goals and targets of the organization's core business activities. Furthermore, characteristics of functional units vary from organization to organization, depending on the business model and size,

Importance

Why is it important to outline core and support functional units when creating an innovation talent recruitment framework? Remember, in the introduction to this book mentioned one of the premises on which it is based: organizations are now seeking to broaden innovation capabilities across functional units. The relevance to innovation talent recruitment is that for the organization to achieve its intention to broaden innovation capabilities, it must have every team member contribute to innovation by having the right numbers and type of innovation skill sets across functional units. One of the factors that vitally contribute to having the right numbers and type of innovation skill sets across functional units is if the leadership has implemented an effective innovation talent recruitment process companywide. Implementing such a process requires review of all functional activities in both core and support function units—and all positions—and then figure out how to integrate innovation performance job descriptions and job specifications in all positions across the functional units.

Illustration of Core and Support Functional Units

Let's take the example of DM Electric, a fictitious company. Assuming DM Electric manufactures a variety of low, medium, and high electrical construction products and has the following product categories:

- Power distribution and control
- Wiring accessories
- Cable and wires
- Transformers
- Lighting

There are two steps. The first is to identify core and support the company's functional units. Let's assume the company has the following functional units:

Core units

- Product development and design department, with the following segments:
  - Power distribution and control
  - Wiring accessories
  - Cable and wires
  - Transformers
  - Lighting
- Manufacturing processes department
- Marketing department, with the following segments:
  - Pricing

- ○ Product delivery process
- ○ New markets
- ○ Product packaging
- ○ Product promotion
- Customer service department

Support unit

- Procurement department
- HR department
- Finance and accounting department
- IT department
- Corporate affairs department

Second is to create simple tables outlining the functional units and various segments of DM Electric. In the example on the following pages, two tables are created.

Table 2-2. Core functional units

Outline of core functional units and functional segments			
Design and product development functional unit	**Manufacturing process functional unit**	**Marketing functional unit**	**Customer service functional unit**
Segments that comprise design and product development department; • Power distribution and control • Wiring accessories • Cable and wires • Transformers • Lighting	**Segments that comprise manufacturing processes department;** • Power distribution and control manufacturing process • Wiring accessories manufacturing process • Cable and wires manufacturing process • Transformers manufacturing process • Lighting manufacturing process	**Segments that comprise Marketing department;** • Pricing • Product delivery process • Promotion • New markets	**Segments that comprise customer service department**
Date of which the outline of functional units was done:			

The table below comprises the support functional units of DM Electric. You will notice that the table does not include an outline of functional activities or components in each support functional unit. In a real scenario, the functional components units would be included.

Table 2-3. Support functional units

Outline of support functional units				
Human Resources	IT	Procurement	Finance and Accounting	Corporate Affairs

Date of which the outline of functional units was done:

Step 4: Understanding the Meaning of Innovation

It is an ineffective endeavour for hiring managers to identify innovation talent without understanding the meaning of innovation, especially in the context of the organization's business model. Thus, step four involves describing the meaning of innovation and how it relates to the organization's innovation talent recruitment process.

Just as understanding the meaning of innovation is critical when undertaking other aspects of innovation management practices in an organization, it is equally so when it comes to sourcing innovation talent. For that reason, this section describes the meaning of innovation in relation to innovation talent recruitment practices by including: (1) the importance of understanding the meaning of innovation in relation to innovation talent recruitment, (2) the definition of innovation (3) the characteristics of innovative ideas.

Importance

There are four reasons why is it important to understand the meaning of innovation in relation to hiring for innovation:

i.   Understanding the meaning of innovation is a vital element in developing the ability to identify and determine innovation skills and abilities in job candidates. The essence of adopting an innovation talent recruitment framework is to ensure that the organization is able to identify and hire candidates with the right innovation skills. How does this relate to the importance of understanding the meaning of innovation? There is no way you can design and implement an effective innovation talent recruitment framework, let alone hire individuals with the right innovation skills, without a broad understanding of the meaning of innovation. That understanding is helpful in appreciating the broad nature or perspectives of innovation performance, and relating that to innovation performance abilities of job candidates, which—as we shall see later—is a critical aspect in identifying and determining innovation skills and abilities in job candidates.

ii. Understanding the meaning of innovation helps to institutionalize the meaning of innovation in the context of the organization's business model. Many people have a misconception about what innovation is, and whose responsibility it is to innovate. For instance, many think innovation is just about the generation of new ideas or all about sophisticated technologies, and others think that only certain professionals or organizational units should be responsible for innovation. I recall a number of instances relating to the misconception of the meaning of innovation, two of which are described here:

In September 2008, I was requested by an organization to develop a training package on innovation performance for the senior management team and board members. The organization requested that I make a presentation to the CEO and six other managers on the contents of the training. At the end of my presentation, one of the managers made an interesting remark: "OK, so this innovation thing is broad. It's not just about new technologies." My response to her was, "You are very right. Innovation is a very broad discipline and that is why it is everybody's business to innovate."

Next, in May 2011, I was walking along Market Street in downtown San Francisco, California, and bumped into an acquaintance I had not seen in a long while. After exchanging greetings and inquiries on what each of us was up to, I somehow found myself telling him about my invention (the CT Holder) and the time frame I had set to have it patented. He looked surprised and asked whether I had studied engineering. I told him you don't need to be an engineer to invent something. "You can do it too," I said to him. The guy was busy shaking his head in disapproval before I could even wind up my encouragement. "I don't think I can do it," he replied.

To institutionalize the meaning of innovation entails adopting an "official" definition of innovation in the context of an organization's business model. This is helpful when it comes to creating the innovation talent recruitment framework because the "official" definition helps to determine how the innovation skills of job candidates fit into the way a company perceives innovation.

Definition

This book defines innovation as a four-part process that involves the following:

Figure 2:1. Definition of innovation

i) Identifying a problem or need (e.g., within a particular customer/market segment or your organizational system)

ii) Generating innovative ideas never seen on the market before to fix the identified problem/need

iv) Converting the innovative solution into monetary value (i.e., in terms of increased revenue or cost reduction)

iii) Transforming the innovative ideas (through an established process) into a solution not seen on the market before

Characteristics of Innovative Ideas

Having described the meaning of innovation, we now look at the characteristics of innovative ideas, which are vital and necessary because unless one understands the characteristics of innovative ideas, it's very difficult to identify an innovative person. That said, the characteristics of innovative ideas have to be understood, especially those involved in talent recruitment.

What, then, are the characteristics of an innovative idea? Based on the definition of innovation, here are some of them:

- New and not seen on the market before

- Aims at meeting customer needs or solving customer problems in a superior manner than before

- Offers benefits to customers in a manner not experienced on the market before

- Should contribute monetary value to the organization

Step 5: Understanding Dimensions of Innovation

We have so far discussed the meaning of innovation and the characteristics of innovative ideas, as well as why it is important to understand these terminologies when it comes to hiring for innovation. Step five looks at the concept of *dimensions of innovation,* and how that relates to the concept of hiring for innovation. To do this, we need to consider the following:(1) definition of dimensions of innovation (2) why it is important to understand dimensions of innovation in relation to creating a framework for hiring for innovation.

Definition

The term dimensions of innovation means that innovation occurs in different contexts of organizational activities; thus, dimensions of innovation describe the different ways in which innovation occurs (i.e., *where*) and the degree of change or newness that innovation entails (i.e., *how*).

In a nutshell, dimensions of innovation is a term that describes two related innovation concepts: types of innovation and innovation degree.

Types of innovation

Remember, dimension of innovation is a concept used to describe two aspects of innovation: *where* and *how* innovation occurs. 'Types of innovation' relates to the context (*where*) in which innovation occurs in the organization's value chain or functional activities. That said, it is vital to understand that innovation occurs in a variety of functional activities across the organization's value chain. For instance, there are innovation ideas (or innovations) in different contexts of products depending on the nature of an organization's product platforms. There are also process innovation ideas depending on the nature of an organization, marketing innovations, customer service innovations, and a whole host of service innovations. Further details about types of innovation are covered in chapter eight in *Leadership for Innovation*, published in 2019 by David Masumba.

Innovation degree

As stated earlier, dimension of innovation is a concept used to describe two aspects of innovation: *where* it occurs and *how* it occurs. We have so far talked about types of innovation, which entails *where* it occurs.

This section looks at *how* innovation occurs in any form or type of innovation, which is referred to as innovation degree, one of the two aspects or concepts of the dimensionality of innovation. This concept is based on how the perception that innovative ideas create or add value in varying degrees or extents. Thus, innovation degree can be defined as the perception of the extent of the newness or novelty of an innovative idea.

Further details on innovation degree are also covered in chapter eight of *Leadership for Innovation*.

Importance

Why is it important to understand how dimensionality of innovation relates to hiring for innovation or talent recruitment process? There are three reasons:

i. Usually, innovation talent is expressed through dimensions of innovation. Remember, the term 'dimensions of innovation' means that innovation occurs in different contexts of organizational activities. Because innovation occurs in a variety of functional activities across the organization's value chain, as described earlier, innovation skills and competencies, therefore, are expressed through innovation-related functional activities that individuals perform in the organization. For instance, marketing professionals would express their innovation abilities by generating or taking part in generating pricing innovative ideas. They would also have the know-how about how pricing innovative ideas are assessed, developed and launched. If those involved in innovation talent recruitment practices or hiring for innovation do not understand what dimensions of innovation entail, it's difficult to create a framework that ensures effective identification of innovation skills and competencies in job candidates, thereby affecting the ability to hire the right number and type of innovation skills and competencies.

ii. It helps job applicants to relate their innovation skills and competencies to the organization's context of dimensions of innovation. Remember, the interpretation of dimensions of innovation is that innovation occurs in a variety of functional activities across the organization's value chain and the organization is supposed to interpret the dimensions of innovation in the context of its value chain, which helps job applicants in a number of ways. For instance, in understanding what dimensions of innovation entails in the context of the organization's value chain, job applicants are able to understand how the organization they are considering joining interprets the dimensions of innovation in relation to its business model. This helps job applicants relate their innovation skills and competencies to the organization's context of dimensions of innovation and, further aiding job applicants to determine whether their competencies and interests match the areas of innovation skills and competencies being sought after by the organization.

iii. An organization needs to have adequate numbers and types of innovation skills if an organization is to succeed in its quest for having a diverse pipeline of innovation ideas across the organization. In order to have a diverse pipeline of innovation ideas, first, the leadership of the organization needs to interpret its dimensions of innovation in a broader way. Second, the leadership needs to build effective capabilities for identifying and hiring the right mixture of innovation talent that will contribute to advancing innovation performance across the organization's business model and value chain by generating various dimensions of innovation ideas. To achieve this, the leadership of the organization should understand what the dimensions of innovation entails in the context of the organization's business model and value chain and how this is reflected in the organization talent recruitment framework and practices.

Step 6: Interpret Meaning of Innovation in the Context of Functional Units

As stated earlier, hiring for innovation is one of the vital practices that contribute to creating a culture for innovation. However, it is important to understand that a culture of innovation is not easy to create in any organization. It's even harder to create a culture of innovation if workforces do not understand the meaning of innovation in the context of the organization's business model and functional units (value chain). For this reason, it is important for the organization to include an aspect of how the meaning of innovation is interpreted in the context of the organization's business model and functional units when creating a framework for hiring for innovation.

That said, step six looks at:(1) the importance of interpreting the meaning of innovation in the context of the organization's business model and functional units and (2) how to interpret the meaning of innovation in the context of the organization's business model and functional units.

Importance

Why is it important to include the meaning of innovation in the context of the organization's business model and functional units when creating a framework for hiring for innovation? There are two reasons:

i. It enhances the ability to identify and hire innovative talent being sought after. Lack of interpretation of the meaning of innovation in the context of the organization business model and functional units could lead to a scenario in which the leadership of the organization has a narrow or unclear understanding of the meaning of innovation. The implication in the context of hiring for innovation is that it affects the leadership's ability to identify and hire innovative talent, and as a result ends up making wrong picks, such as candidates with inadequate or incorrect innovation skills. In other words, how do you hire innovative talent if you have no clear understanding of the meaning of innovation in the context of your organization to begin with? It's certainly difficult to do ! For instance, if a company is in manufacturing and has no clear and simple interpretation of the company's "process innovation," it will be difficult to identify talent with manufacturing-process innovative thinking skills. Therefore, interpreting innovation in the context of functional units is important because it enhances the capacity to identify and hire talent with the right mixture of innovation skills and competencies across functional units.

ii. Interpreting the meaning of innovation in the context of the functional units enables prospective job applicants to understand, beforehand, how the organization interprets the meaning of innovation. This helps prospective job applicants think through and gauge how they can apply themselves to contribute toward advancing innovation across functional units if they were to join the organization.

How to Translate the Meaning of Innovation

Based on the reasons advanced in the preceding section, it is important to state and understand the meaning of innovation in the context of the organization's business model and functional units when creating the framework for hiring for innovation. The question is, how do you translate the meaning of innovation in the context of the organization's business model and functional units? Chapter eight (*Institutionalizing and Educating Workforces about the Meaning of Innovation*) of *Leadership for Innovation* has a detailed section on how to translate the meaning of innovation in the context of the organization's business model and functional units.

Chapter Three

ESSENTIAL ELEMENTS

Overview

Remember, the introduction to this book states that it's structured in thirteen steps on how to create a framework for hiring for innovation. Chapter two covered the first six steps. Chapter three looks at the next four steps:

- Step 7: Understanding factors driving innovation

- Step 8: Review job positions, and create innovation performance job descriptions and job specifications

- Step 9: Creating innovation goals

- Step 10: Interpreting innovation skills

Step 7: Understanding Factors Driving Innovation

Usually, the need for innovation strategy in companies is mainly influenced by both internal and external factors. As part of the process for creating a framework for hiring for innovation, it is important for the company to include a component of *how* and *why* comprehension of internal and external factors is essential to the innovation talent recruitment process. This section includes: (1) definition of internal and external factors (2) why it's important to understand internal and external factors influencing innovation in the organization when creating a framework for hiring for innovation, (3) how to determine and use the internal and external factors driving innovation in functional units.

Definition of Internal and External Factors

We define internal and external factors as factors obtainable within the organization and in the business environment that, in one way or another, affect the organization's existence, activities and future direction, and therefore, influence innovation decisions of an organization. Chapter eight (*Educating Workforces about the Drivers of Innovation*) in *Leadership for Innovation* includes numerous examples of internal and external factors that influence organizations to implement strategies to advance innovation across functional units.

Importance

Why is it important to understand internal and external factors influencing innovation in the organization when creating the framework for hiring for innovation? There are two reasons:

   i.   It is helpful in determining the type and level of innovation skills and competencies required by job candidates to match the innovation performance requirements. As stated earlier, the essence of creating a framework for hiring for innovation is to identify and hire candidates with the right level of innovation skills to contribute toward advancing innovation performance across functional units in sync with the strategic direction of an organization. So the importance of understanding the connection between hiring for innovation and internal and external factors is that it helps the leadership of the organization and those involved in the hiring process to effectively determine the type and level of innovation skills and competencies required by job candidates to match the innovation performance requirements of particular positions in light of certain internal or external factors influencing innovation in the organization.

ii. Not only is understanding the connection between hiring for innovation and internal and external factors driving innovation important to talent recruiters, it also is important to job applicants, in that job applicants will grasp some aspects of various internal and external factors that are influencing the leadership of the organization to emphasize innovation performance across functional units. Once job applicants have a grasp of the factors, they'll use the information to gauge their suitability for innovation performance in the job positions to which they aspire. And they will use the information to argue their case on why and how they meet the innovation performance requirements of the position. The candidates could, for instance, argue by highlighting some cues for innovation performance opportunities that they are able to identify from the various internal and external factors that the company has described. Thus, it is important for the leadership to ensure that information about internal and external factors driving innovation in the company is publicized (on the company website and in brochures) and should be easily accessed by job applicants.

The table below is an example of how internal and external factors can be applied in functional units for hiring for innovation.

Table 3-1. Application of internal and external factors

Name of department:
Category of the department *core* or *support* functional unit:
Position:
Date of which assessment of factors is being conducted:

Internal and external factors driving innovation in the functional unit	Outline required innovation skill sets in light of the stated internal and external factors of the organization		
	Innovative thinking skills	Innovation engagement skills	Innovation management skills
Names and position of staff conducting assessment:			

Step 8: Review Job Position, and Create Innovation Performance Job Descriptions and Job Specifications

The purpose of hiring innovation talent is for such talent to execute the required level of innovation performance that the individuals are hired for—also contribute to achieving innovation goals of their functional unit and, ultimately, contribute to meeting overall innovation goals of the organization. Innovation performance does not happen in a vacuum; it is enacted by workforces in the form of performance by undertaking specific innovation-related tasks. That being said, there is a need for guidelines on how job applicants are expected to execute innovation performance in the context of the job positions they have applied for. These guidelines are in the form of job positions, job descriptions, and job specifications. This is where step eight comes in as part of the process of creating a framework for hiring for innovation. The step looks at reviewing position titles and creating innovation performance job descriptions and job specifications across functional units in relation to creating or conducting a process for hiring job applicants for innovation.

That being said, the following aspects include: (1) the meaning of innovation performance job descriptions and innovation performance job specifications, (2) why it's important to review position titles, create innovation performance job descriptions and job specifications, (3) reviewing current job descriptions and job specifications in each functional unit, (4) and examples of how to outline a position title, innovation performance job description, and job specification.

Definition

What does innovation performance job descriptions and job specifications mean? In a nutshell, it is a conjoint terminology that shows an outline of innovation-related duties and responsibilities and innovation-related job specifications, such as characteristics, abilities, knowledge, and experience needed to perform innovation performance–related duties and responsibilities. For elaborate details on this topic, chapter eight of *Leadership for Innovation* provides a detailed explanation of innovation performance job descriptions and job specifications.

Importance

Why is it important to review job positions and create innovation performance job descriptions and job specifications when hiring for innovation? There are two reasons:

i. It helps in identifying job candidates with the required innovation skills and competencies. It's important to bear in mind that innovation performance in organizations does not take place in a vacuum; it's enacted by workforces in the form of performance by undertaking specific innovation-related tasks. In relation to hiring for innovation, it means that without guidelines in terms of innovation-related duties and responsibilities and innovation-related requirements, it is difficult to identify job candidates with the right type of innovation skill sets needed for the job. In other words, if innovation-performance duties and requirements are not stated or specified in the hiring process, the hiring of innovation talent is left to chance—and the chances of hiring individuals with the right innovation talents that the position needs are pretty low.

ii. It provides vital data that can be applied in the decision making of the innovation-talent hiring process.

Recall that the purpose of hiring innovation talent is for such talent to execute required level of innovation performance and contribute to achieving functional unit innovation goals that contribute to meeting overall innovation goals of the organization and, ultimately, lead to realizing the organization vision. However, job holders cannot meaningfully execute required levels of innovation performance without innovation performance guidelines. So conducting job position reviews, and reviewing the innovation-performance duties and requirements in relation to the process of hiring for innovation enables you to understand important innovation performance duties of the position, how they are carried out, and the necessary innovation skills and competencies needed to carry them out. This provides vital data that informs the innovation-talent hiring process.

iii. It helps in ensuring that the innovation performance duties and requirements are accurately outlined for purposes of effective interview questions. Remember, the purpose of creating a framework for hiring for innovation is to ensure that the organization has an effective capability to identify, assess and determine innovation skills and competencies in job candidates. However, the effectiveness of the whole process of innovation talent recruitment in terms of making the right innovation talent picks hinges, among other factors, on the accuracy of the innovation performance job descriptions and job specifications which provide critical information resources used to formulate and phrase innovation performance related interview questions. And these questions elicit data that is applied to identify and determine the right innovation skills and competencies in job applicants. What this means is that if the innovation performance job descriptions and job specifications are inaccurate, there is a high risk of formulating wrong interview questions, which will lead to eliciting wrong answers, and ultimately, result in hiring unsuitable candidates in relation to the needs of the innovation performance duties and responsibilities of a job position.

Aspects to Consider When Reviewing and Creating Innovation Performance Job Descriptions and Job Specifications

Here are some steps to consider when reviewing and creating innovation performance job descriptions and job specifications in each functional unit for purposes of hiring for innovation:

Review Current Job Descriptions and Job Specifications

Use simple tools to outline current job descriptions and job specifications in all job positions across functional units. Here is a table that can be used for that purpose.

Table 3-2. Example of a table for outlining current job descriptions and job specifications

Name of department: Position title:	
Summary of the current job description	Summary of the current job specification
Date of which review was conducted:	
Position of staff or committee that conducted the review:	

Ask Relevant Questions

This step involves asking pertinent questions in the context of job descriptions and job specifications of a particular job position. For instance, questions such as:

Job descriptions

- Does the job position require the job holder to undertake all the three categories of innovation performance responsibilities: (1) innovative thinking-related duties (2) innovation engagement-related duties, and (3) innovation management-related duties?

- What innovation performance related responsibilities do you need to enhance/add on or subtract from the current job descriptions, taking into account various aspects such as: the corporate strategy of the organization, changes in the business environment and future scenarios driving innovation in the particular functional unit and the organization as a whole organization?

- Job Specification of the categories of innovation abilities listed below, which of the category of abilities is the job holder required to possess?

  - Innovative thinking abilities

  - Innovation engagement abilities

  - Innovation management abilities

  All the above abilities (later in this book, we've provided tools for determining necessity of the innovation abilities for each job position).

Formulate Innovation Performance Job Descriptions and Job Specifications

Once the review job descriptions and job specifications are done, next is creating innovation performance duties and responsibilities (job description) and innovation performance job specifications:

- *Understand the meaning of innovation performance duties and innovation performance requirements:* Remember, this was defined as an outline of innovation-related duties and responsibilities and innovation-related job specifications, such as characteristics, abilities, knowledge, and experience needed to perform innovation performance–related duties and responsibilities. Again, for elaborate details on this topic, chapter eight of my book, titled *"Leadership for Innovation"*, has provided a detailed meaning of innovation performance job descriptions and job specifications.

- *Create a tool for outlining innovation performance job description and job specification:* On next page is an example of a table that can be used to outline innovation performance job descriptions and job specifications of each job position across functional units. Information about innovation performance can be obtained using different methods such as interviews with incumbent job holders, interviews with supervisors, panels of organization's leadership, structured questionnaires, revised outline of tasks, and duties and responsibilities.

Step 9: Creating Functional Unit Innovation Goals

One of the indicators of a culture of innovation in an organization is the formulation of various contexts of innovation goals across functional units. Innovation goals play a vital role in helping organizational leaders make decisions about the type and level of innovation skill sets needed across functional units. Thus, the major reason for sourcing innovation talent is to meet innovation performance needs of the organization which are expressed in terms of achieving functional unit and

Table 3-3. Categories of innovation performance duties and requirements

Name of department:		
Position title:		
State whether position title is *limited* or *generic*:		
If *generic*, indicate number of position titles:		
Three categories of innovation performance duties		
Innovative thinking-related duties and responsibilities	Innovation engagement-related duties and responsibilities	Innovation management-related duties & responsibilities
Categories of innovation performance job requirements		
Innovative thinking abilities	Innovation engagement abilities	Innovation management abilities
Name of staff or committee responsible for creating the innovation performance job description and job specification summary:		
Date of which the outline was created:		

corporate innovation goals, which ultimately contribute to realizing the organization vision.

Step 9 looks at the importance of understanding functional innovation goals in relation to hiring for innovation: (1) definition of innovation goals, (2) why it is important to understand innovation goals in relation to hiring for innovation.

Definition

Innovation goals are statements expressing the desired future state of innovation performance to be attained within a specified period in the context of the specified level of the organization (i.e., individual level, departmental level, corporate level).

Importance

Why is it important to understand innovation goals in relation to hiring for innovation?

The following are three reasons:

i.   It helps in hiring the right innovation talent to realize organizational vision. Remember, formulation of innovation goals across functional units of an organization is one of the indicators of a culture of innovation. In terms of hiring for innovation, the importance of understanding functional unit innovation goals is that once the leadership formulates functional unit innovation goals, the next step is to come up with effective methods and techniques to accurately identify and hire the right number and type of innovation talent needed by the organization to achieve short and long term functional unit innovation goals that will contribute to achieving corporate innovation goals and, ultimately, realize the organization vision.

ii. Prospective job candidates will have an idea about the future innovation aspiration of the organization. Not only is the understanding of innovation performance important to hiring managers, but also to job candidates. With that, job applicants will have an idea of the future innovation performance aspirations and targets that the organization leadership has set across functional units. And job applicants will be able to use the information regarding innovation goals to argue their case about their suitability for the job and how they'll contribute to achieving the short- and long-term innovation goals of the functional unit (and of the organization as a whole). Furthermore, it's important for the leadership to ensure that information about the organization's innovation performance goals is put out (either on the company website or in brochures) and should be easily accessed by prospective job applicants to use for purposes of employment with the company.

iii. Innovation goals provide data for formulating questions. The ability to identify and determine the right innovation skills and competencies in job candidates depend on the ability of the hiring team to elicit valuable data from job applicants. The elicitation of data hinges on the effectiveness of both the techniques and questions used to elicit innovation abilities-related data from job candidates. With the importance of understanding innovation goals, questions on innovation abilities are usually formulated and phrased based on various aspects of innovation practices. And one of the key practices useful for formulating innovation questions is functional unit and corporate innovation goals.

Step 10: Interpreting the Innovation Skill Sets

Over the years, business experts, corporate leaders, and academic researchers across industries have consistently said that innovation is an attainable skill that can be developed, adopted and applied across industries. This book has adopted three categories of innovation skill sets—namely, innovative thinking skills, innovation engagement skills and innovation management skills. So, the tenth step of creating the process for hiring innovation involves two things: one, *interpreting the three categories of innovation skill sets*, and two, *how the three skill sets relate to the hiring or recruiting of innovation talent.* This step covers: (1) the definition of innovation skill, (2) why it's important to understand innovation skills in relation to hiring innovation talent, and (3) how and where to apply innovation skills.

Definition of Innovation Skills

Before we look at the meaning, it's important to state the obvious that whether in the financial industry, insurance, health, hospitality, hotel, media, entertainment, food, telecommunications or manufacturing, innovation skills can be applied in all industries. So, we define innovation skills as a combination of abilities that individuals can attain and apply in a particular organizational context to carry out innovation performance duties and responsibilities—and contribute to advancing innovation performance in an organization.

Importance

Why is it important to understand innovation skills in relation to hiring innovation talent? Two reasons:

i. You can't hire innovation talent if you have no clue about innovation skills: Like any type of skills, innovation skills are expressible, assessable, and can be determined within a desired context. Determination of the right innovation skills is the core element and goal in hiring for innovation. However, it is almost impossible to identify and determine job candidates with the right innovation skills or innovation talent if to start with, individuals involved in the hiring process for innovation talent do not understand the meaning of innovation skills and attributes—also how they can be translated in the context of the organization's business model, functional units, and particular position titles.

ii. It enables recruiters to clearly describe the innovation abilities required in a particular job. Remember, innovation performance does not happen in a vacuum, it is enacted by workforces in the form of performance by undertaking specific innovation-related tasks. How is this related to hiring for innovation? In order for workforces to execute innovation performance activities they, conversely, must possess the right and required level of innovation skill sets to execute the innovation tasks. For recruiters to attract the right innovation talent they must be able to understand the context of innovation skill sets require in the job position. However, hiring managers will only be able to correctly outline required innovation abilities if they understand broadly about the required innovation skills in the context of the organization's value chain and to the specific job position. Outlining required innovation abilities correctly is also very beneficial to job candidates, in that it helps job candidates to examine and express themselves in how their innovation abilities compare with the innovation skill requirements of the position being filled—thereby, making it easy for the recruiters to determine whether or not the job candidate meets the innovation skill requirements for the position.

The introduction of *Leadership for Innovation* provides a detailed description of the categories of innovation skill sets.

Application of Innovation Skills

Where and how should you apply innovation skills? As stated earlier, innovation skills can be applied across industries: finance, insurance, health, hospitality, media, entertainment, food, telecommunication, manufacturing and so on. Innovation skills can also be applied by any anyone across functional units of organizations. Based on how broad-based innovation skills can be applied, innovation in many organizations is now perceived as everyone's responsibility from the most junior in the organization to the CEO. However, the value of contribution to innovation performance by workforces depends on the level and type of innovation skill sets they possess and how those innovation abilities are applied. To this end, it is important for hiring managers to understand the different contexts of innovation skill sets and how they are applied across functional units and specific job positions.

This also means that for an organization to generate high value benefits from innovation skills, everyone across functional units of the organization must understand the contexts in which they discharge their innovation performance, without which workforces will have difficulties in discharging the innovation performance duties. And this can hinder the organization from benefitting from the innovation talents across functional units. That said, we've adopted three categories of innovation skill sets: innovative thinking skills, innovation engagement skills and innovation management skills. To answer the question we asked earlier, *how are innovation skills applied?*

Once obtained, innovations skills can be applied to perform innovation functional activities in accordance with the categories of innovation skill sets outlined above. Innovative thinking skills will be responsible for executing innovative thinking-related functional activities, innovation engagement skills will be responsible for executing innovation engagement-related functional activities, and innovation management skills will be responsible for executing innovation management-related functional activities.

Understanding the Types of Innovation Skill Sets

Remember, the value of contribution to innovation performance by workforces depends on the level and type of innovation skill set that they possess and how the innovation abilities are applied. In order for hiring managers to identify and hire job candidates with the level and type of innovation skill sets that will contribute meaningful innovation performance to the functional unit, it's important for hiring managers to understand the different contexts of innovation skill sets and how these skill sets can be translated and applied across functional units and in specific job positions.

Here, we look at the three categories of innovation skill sets and how they can be harnessed to hire individuals with the right innovation talents. In the following we describe how each of the three skill sets can be harnessed or translated to identify, assess, and hire job candidates with the right innovation talents for experienced positions.

i. Innovative Thinking Skills

There are three aspects to look for when you are determining innovative thinking skills:

- First, the *ability to identify problems:* This involves the ability for the job candidates to identify problems, needs, and challenges in the context of the organization's business model, the context of the functional activities, and the job position. Remember, innovative thinking skills can be expressed and applied across industries, as those stated earlier—financial, insurance, health, hospitality, hotel, media, entertainment, food, telecommunication and manufacturing. So, you should be looking at the candidates' ability to identify problems, needs, and challenges in the context of their past job experiences and how they will be able to translate their past innovation-related functional activities into the job activities they are applying for.

- Second, the *ability to turn problems into innovation opportunities:* This involves determining the ability of the job candidates to turn the needs and the problems into innovation opportunities by *generating new ideas* or solutions (i.e. solutions not seen on the market before) to fix the identified problem or need. Information about this ability can be obtained by *formulating* and *asking questions* aimed at eliciting responses that are easily interpreted to determine whether the job candidate possess this ability in the context of the functional unit and the specific job position.

- Third, *innovative attributes:* These are character traits or personal qualities that an innovative thinking person can attain and possess and help them drive their innovative performance in a variety of contexts.

Here is a list of examples of how to harness innovative attributes to identify, assess, and hire job candidates with the right innovative thinking skills.

- **Questioning attribute:** Formulate questions that will help job candidates reveal whether they possess the questing attribute, i.e. whether the job candidate has the attributes that constantly question the *what, why,* and the *how* about something. Let them express themselves how they have used this attribute in functional activities. Formulate questions to elicit information on how job candidates have harnessed their questioning attributes to find alternative ways to solve a problem or do something in their functional activities.

- **Problem-solving attribute:** Formulate questions to elicit information on how job candidates have used their problem-solving attributes to generate ideas for creating new value in their functional activities.

- **No fear-for-failure attribute:** Formulate questions aimed at eliciting information from job candidates about how they perceive failure in relation to generating innovative ideas.

- **Networking attribute:** Studies have revealed that one of the attributes of innovative people is networking. Formulate questions aimed at eliciting information from job candidates about their networking activities and how such activities have help shape their innovative thinking skills.

- **Associating attributes**: Formulate questions aimed at eliciting information from job candidates about their associating attributes, i.e. information that reveals a pattern of behaviour that involves a constant practice of engaging in interlacing and combining ideas from from different areas or fields to solve a particular problem or improve upon the existing solutions.

- **Observation attributes:** Formulate questions aimed at eliciting information from job candidates about innovation-related observation abilities. Aim at eliciting real-life from the job candidates about how they have used their observation abilities to identify a need or problem and how they've used it (observing attribute) to generate an innovative idea.

- **Experimenting attributes:** Formulate questions aimed at eliciting information from job candidates about their experimenting attributes, i.e. what kind of approaches and techniques do the candidates engage in to practice enhancing their experimenting attributes.

- **Envisioning attributes:** In the organizational context, envisioning is the ability to understand, predict, or picture key aspects of market (local or global) trends or patterns that affect the organization's business trends. Formulate questions aimed at eliciting information from job candidates about their envisioning attribute.

- **Risk taking attributes:** Formulate questions aimed at eliciting information from job candidates about their risking-taking attributes.

- **Challenging status quo attributes:** Formulate questions aimed at eliciting information from job candidates about whether they possess the attribute for challenging status quo for improvement purposes.

- **Experiential learning attributes:** Formulate questions aimed at eliciting information from job candidates about the attribute of learning from past experiences and how they have applied their past experience to generate innovative ideas.

ii. Innovation Engagement Skills

The significance of innovation engagement skills in hiring for innovation is dependent upon the leadership roles performed in a job position, normally for experienced hires. This means that innovation engagement skills will be required more in job positions that have a number of leadership roles. Thus, the more leadership roles a job position possesses, the more innovation engagement skills will be required. That said, there are a number of innovation engagement abilities that can be identified and determined depending on the scale and level of leadership roles of a position. A number of innovation experts have said innovation is a mind-set that should pervade the whole organization, therefore, leaders must possess skills for engaging passion, emotional interest, and commitment to advance innovation across the organization.

Here is a list of examples of how to harness various aspects of innovation engagement abilities to identify and determine job candidates with the right level of innovation engagement skills for the job position.

- Formulate questions aimed at eliciting information from job candidates about their abilities to regularly educate and inspire workforces (e.g., at meetings, conferences, or retreats; also in brochures, articles, and newsletters) in terms of the vision of the company.

- Formulate questions aimed at eliciting information from job candidates about their abilities to articulate and communicate various innovation-support initiatives—such as innovation strategies, innovation policies/procedures/plans, innovation goals, and innovation targets—implemented in the organization.

- Formulate questions aimed at eliciting information from job candidates about their abilities to articulate and communicate (in simple and clear terms) the innovation performance of the company in each functional unit or division and in terms of the organization as a whole.

- Formulate questions aimed at eliciting information from job candidates on their involvement in educating workforces about various aspects of innovation, such as the meaning of innovation, types of innovation, and the significance of innovation to an organization.

- Formulate questions aimed at eliciting information from job candidates about their abilities to formulate innovation-motivating slogans, catchphrases, and visual illustrations aimed at contributing toward instilling innovation performance in the hearts and minds of workforces.

- Formulate questions aimed at eliciting information from job candidates about their abilities to create techniques to effectively communicate innovation-motivating slogans, catchphrases, and visual illustrations aimed at instilling innovation performance in the hearts and minds of workforces.

- Formulate questions aimed at eliciting information from job candidates about their abilities to exhibit fit-for-purpose attitudes, language, and actions aimed at contributing toward creating an organizational climate that encourages innovative thinking across the organization.

Part three of *Leadership for Innovation* has a detailed description of a number of aspects about the role of innovation engagement skills in creating a culture of innovation in organizations.

iii. Innovation Management Skills

As in innovation engagement skills, the significance of innovation management skills in hiring for innovation is dependent on the leadership roles performed in a job position—again, normally for experienced hires. This means that innovation management skills will be required more in job positions that have a number of leadership roles. Thus, the more leadership roles a job position possesses, the more innovation management skills will be required. That being said, there are a number of innovation management abilities that can be identified and determined depending on the scale and level of leadership roles of a position.

Innovation management skills are based on the understanding that you cannot create a culture of innovation across the organization using traditional, non-innovation oriented management tools. So, if you are looking for job candidates who will be required to take part in creating innovation-support systems, then you need tools and techniques for identifying and determining innovation management skills in job candidates. We define innovation management skills as: *the ability to formulate and implement innovation-support systems.* What are innovation-support systems? These are the innovation-support strategies, policies and procedures, and structures aimed at contributing to advancing the culture of innovation across the organization. When you are recruiting for individuals who will be involved in driving innovation from a leadership perspective, you need job candidates with the ability to create some innovation-support systems.

It's important to mention here that innovation management skills are very context dependent. What this means is that the innovation management skills will vary in context depending on the nature of functional activities and the job position. That being said, here is how you would contextualize innovation management skills if you are hiring for job positions in the following functional activities: *product unit "X", marketing unit, HR unit, and accounting and finance unit.*

   i. **Job position for a product unit "X":** Assume you are looking for a qualified person to fill a leadership role in a product unit "X" for a fictitious company. Here is a list of examples of how you would harness various aspects of innovation management abilities to identify and determine job candidates with the right level of innovation management skills for the job position.

- Formulate questions aimed at eliciting information from job candidates about their abilities to create innovation-performance job duties and responsibilities.

- Formulate questions aimed at eliciting information from job candidates about their abilities to develop and implement product innovation strategies.

- Formulate questions aimed at eliciting information from job candidates about their abilities to create product innovation goals.

- Formulate questions aimed at eliciting information from job candidates about their abilities to generate innovation-challenge questions for product units.

- Formulate questions aimed at eliciting information from job candidates about their abilities to design and implement a system for management of innovation ideas for product units.

- Formulate questions aimed at eliciting information from job candidates about their abilities to structure and report innovation performance for product units.

ii. **Job position for a marketing unit:** Assume you are looking for a qualified person to fill a leadership role in a marketing unit for a fictitious company. Here is a list of examples of how you would harness various aspects of innovation management abilities to identify and determine job candidates with the right level of innovation management skills for the job position.

- Formulate questions aimed at eliciting information from job candidates about their abilities to develop and implement marketing innovation strategies for various product platforms.

- Formulate questions aimed at eliciting information from job candidates about their abilities to create marketing innovation goals.

- Formulate questions aimed at eliciting information from job candidates about their abilities to generate marketing innovation-challenge questions for product-based segments.

- Formulate questions aimed at eliciting information from job candidates about their abilities to design, implement, and sustain an effective framework for assessing, analyzing, and enacting innovative marketing ideas.

- Formulate questions aimed at eliciting information from job candidates about their abilities to structure and report marketing innovation performance.

- Formulate questions aimed at eliciting information from job candidates about their abilities to create innovation-centered marketing duties and responsibilities.

iii. **Job position for an HR unit:** Assume you are looking for a qualified person to fill a leadership role in an HR unit for a fictitious company. Here is a list of examples of how you would harness various aspects of innovation management abilities to identify and determine job candidates with the right level of innovation management skills for the job position.

- Formulate questions aimed at eliciting information from job candidates about their abilities to create duties and responsibilities for HR innovation-performance support.

- Formulate questions aimed at eliciting information from job candidates about their abilities develop and implement strategies for HR innovation-performance support, such as the following:
  ○ Strategy for recruitment of innovation talent
  ○ Strategy for workforce innovation-performance appraisal and reward
  ○ Framework for innovation-talent-succession planning
  ○ Strategy for innovation-talent development
  ○ Strategy for workforce diversity

- Formulate questions aimed at eliciting information from job candidates about their abilities to create goals for HR innovation-performance support.

- Formulate questions aimed at eliciting information from job candidates about their abilities to generate innovation-challenge questions related to HR innovation-performance support.

- Formulate questions aimed at eliciting information from job candidates about their abilities to structure and report initiatives and activities for HR innovation-performance support.

Innovative HR cost-saving skills

- Formulate questions aimed at eliciting information from job candidates about their abilities to create innovative HR cost-saving duties and responsibilities.

- Formulate questions aimed at eliciting information from job candidates about their abilities to create innovative HR cost-saving goals.

- Formulate questions aimed at eliciting information from job candidates about their abilities to design, implement, and sustain an effective framework for assessing, analyzing, and enacting innovative HR cost-saving ideas.

iv. **Job position for finance and accounting unit:** Assume you are looking for a qualified person to fill a leadership role in the finance and accounting unit for a fictitious company. Here is a list of examples of how you would harness various aspects of innovation management abilities to identify and determine job candidates with the right level of innovation management skills for the job position.

- Formulate questions aimed at eliciting information from job candidates about their abilities to create duties and responsibilities for finance and accounting innovation-performance support.

- Formulate questions aimed at eliciting information from job candidates about their abilities to develop and implement strategies for finance and accounting innovation-performance support.

- Formulate questions aimed at eliciting information from job candidates about their abilities to create goals for finance and accounting innovation-performance support.

- Formulate questions aimed at eliciting information from job candidates about their abilities to create innovation-challenge questions for finance and accounting innovation-performance support.

- Formulate questions aimed at eliciting information from job candidates about their abilities to structure and report initiatives and activities for finance and accounting innovation-performance support.

- Formulate questions aimed at eliciting information from job candidates about their abilities to create duties and responsibilities centered on innovative cost savings in finance and accounting.

Innovative finance and accounting cost-saving skills

- Formulate questions aimed at eliciting information from job candidates about their abilities to create goals for finance and accounting innovative cost savings

- Formulate questions aimed at eliciting information from job candidates about their abilities to design, implement, and sustain an effective framework for assessing, analyzing, and enacting innovative ideas for finance and accounting cost savings.

Part three of *Leadership for Innovation* provides a detailed description of various examples of innovation management skills (see Expression of Innovation Management Skills).

Chapter Four

TOOLS FOR IDENTIFYING INNOVATION SKILLS AND COMPETENCIES IN EXPERIENCED HIRES

Overview

Remember, the introduction of this book cited a number of studies about talent shortages across the globe; and according, to these studies, the situation seems to be escalating.

Furthermore, we cited a 2016 study by a US-based talent recruitment company stating that talent shortage is hurting innovation across industries, and this was affecting the revenues of organizations across industries due to slowdowns in market expansion and product development. In today's innovation-driven economy, in which competitors hire diverse innovation talent, finding job candidates with the right innovation skills is very difficult. It's even harder if an organization has no tools with which to identify the right innovation talent. The preceding two chapters have described essential aspects to understanding creating an effective mechanism for hiring for innovation. This chapter looks at the next two steps:

- Step 11: Rating mechanism for determining importance of innovation skills in experienced hires

- Step 12: Tools for identifying innovation skills and competencies in experienced hires

Step 11: Rating Mechanism for Determining Importance of Innovation Skills in Experienced Hires

Remember, when discussing the element of reviewing job positions and creating innovation performance job descriptions and job specifications (step 8), we said that each job position has a different scope of demands of innovation performance duties and responsibilities, and by the same token, vary in innovation skill and competence requirements. For instance, position "X" may have innovation performance functional activities that are centered more on innovative thinking-related duties and responsibilities as opposed to innovation engagement-related duties or innovation management-related duties. On the other hand, position "Y" may have innovation performance functional activities that are centered more on innovation engagement-related duties and innovation management-related duties, than innovative thinking-related duties. What does this imply?

The implication is that the leadership has to implement the right tools to effectively identify and hire job candidates with the right innovation skills and competencies to achieve the goal of building an innovation talent pool with the right mixture of innovation skill sets across functional units. One such a tool is the *innovation skills rating scale*. The innovation skills rating scale is used to assess and determine criticalness of each category or type of innovation ability in relation to innovation performance demands of the job position.

Innovation Skills Rating Scale

We have categorized the innovation skills rating scale according to all the three types of the innovation skill sets stated below:

- Scale i: Criticality of innovative thinking skills
- Scale ii: Criticality of innovation engagement skills
- Scale iii: Criticality of innovation management skills

Nex page is an example of simple innovation skills rating scales (i.e. scale i, ii, & iii), for determining criticality of each of the above three types of innovation skill sets and how the rating question could be phrased.

Table: 4.1. Scale i: Criticality of innovative thinking skills

<table>
<tr><td colspan="6">Position title:----------------------- Department:-----------------------------</td></tr>
<tr><td rowspan="4">Criticality of innovative thinking skills in the position under consideration</td><td>Not critical</td><td>Slightly Critical</td><td>Moderately Critical</td><td>Very Critical</td><td>Extremely Critical</td></tr>
<tr><td>1</td><td>2</td><td>3</td><td>4</td><td>5</td></tr>
<tr><td colspan="5">Indicate the rating in the box below and reasons for the choice of the rating</td></tr>
<tr><td colspan="5"></td></tr>
</table>

Table: 4.2. Scale ii: Criticality of innovation engagement skills

<table>
<tr><td colspan="6">Position title:-------------------- Department:----------------------------</td></tr>
<tr><td rowspan="4">Criticality of innovation engagement skills in the position under consideration</td><td>Not critical</td><td>Slightly Critical</td><td>Moderately Critical</td><td>Very Critical</td><td>Extremely Critical</td></tr>
<tr><td>1</td><td>2</td><td>3</td><td>4</td><td>5</td></tr>
<tr><td colspan="5">Indicate the rating in the box below and reasons for the choice of the rating</td></tr>
<tr><td colspan="5"></td></tr>
</table>

Table 4.3. Scale iii: Criticality of innovation management skills

<table>
<tr><td colspan="6">Position title:----------------------- Department:---------------------------</td></tr>
<tr><td rowspan="4">Criticality of innovation management skills in the position under consideration</td><td>Not critical</td><td>Slightly Critical</td><td>Moderately Critical</td><td>Very Critical</td><td>Extremely Critical</td></tr>
<tr><td>1</td><td>2</td><td>3</td><td>4</td><td>5</td></tr>
<tr><td colspan="5">Indicate the rating in the box below and reasons for the choice of the rating</td></tr>
<tr><td colspan="5"></td></tr>
</table>

How to Apply the Rating Scales

Remember, the rating scales are used to determine criticality of each type of innovation skill set in relation to innovation performance demands of a job position. In order to determine criticality of each type of innovation skill set in relation to the position, the innovation performance job description and specification of the position under consideration should be reviewed for purposes of rating the criticality of the innovation skill set for the job position under consideration. This should be followed by stating the rating decision by indicating the appropriate rating number as provided in the rating scale above.

Next step involves creating tools for identifying innovation skills and competencies in job candidates.

Step 12: Tools for Identifying Innovation Skills in Experienced Hires

Again, it is difficult to hire innovation talent that the organization requires to meet its innovation needs without the right tools. In this section we look at some of the tools and processes that are essential for identifying job candidates with the right innovation skills and competencies. Here is a list of the tools:

1. Job Applicant Innovation Competencies Elicitation Form

2. Innovation Competencies Selection Process

3. Innovation Competencies Selection Interview

4. Candidate Innovation Competencies Assessment Worksheet

5. Post-Innovation Competencies Selection Interview

6. Reconciling *Non-Innovation Competencies* and the *Innovation Competencies* to Make A Selection Decision

Each of the above is described as follows:

1. **Job Applicant Innovation Competencies Elicitation Form**

   This would be the first tool for eliciting information from job candidates regarding their innovation abilities and competencies. Since hiring for innovation is a supplementary selection procedure, usually done after the candidate is interviewed for the main technical skills, job candidates should fill out two application forms—that is, the technical professional skills-centered application form and the innovation skills-centered one, referred to in this book as the Job Applicant Innovation Competencies Elicitation Form (i.e. JAICE form). A committee or taskforce could be established by the leadership to design the JAICE form. An example JAICE form is provided below. The form is divided into three parts. Each part focuses on eliciting data about particular innovation skills and competencies. Here is an outline of each of the types of innovation skill sets included in the JAICE form.

   - Determining innovation thinking skills and competencies–part 1

   - Determination of innovation engagement skills–part 2

   - Determination of innovation management skills–part 3

Each of the innovation skill sets has a rating scale that job candidates can apply to rate their abilities and competencies against, by marking "X" on any of the rating options provided in each of the innovation-related skill sets appearing on the form.

Table 4.3. Example of job applicant innovation competencies elicitation form

Job Applicant Innovation Competencies Elicitation Form (JAICE Form)
Name of job applicant:
Position title being applied for:
Name of department:
Date when form was filled:
Phone #:
E-mail:

<table>
<tr><td colspan="2" align="center">

Part 1
Determining Innovative Thinking Skills

Interpretation: State the meaning of innovative thinking skills in the context of the organization. For instance, you could interpret it as *the ability for the job candidates to identify problems, needs, and challenges; being able to turn the needs and the problems into innovation opportunities by generating new ideas or solutions (i.e. solutions not seen on the market before) to fix the identified problem or need.*

Rating scale: Job candidates rate themselves against the innovative thinking skills and attributes outlined below.

</td></tr>
<tr><td>

Rating scale for innovative thinking skills

</td><td>

Evidence by job candidate to support their rating choice

</td></tr>
<tr><td>

Questioning attribute

Poor	Fair	Good	Excellent
1	2	3	4

</td><td>

Evidence from job candidate to back–up their rating in this category

</td></tr>
<tr><td>

Problem-solving attribute

Poor	Fair	Good	Excellent
1	2	3	4

</td><td>

Evidence from job candidate to back up their rating in this category

</td></tr>
<tr><td>

No fear-for-failure attribute

Poor	Fair	Good	Excellent
1	2	3	4

</td><td>

Evidence from job candidate provided to back up their rating in this category

</td></tr>
<tr><td>

Networking attribute

Poor	Fair	Good	Excellent
1	2	3	4

</td><td>

Evidence from job candidate to back up their rating in this category

</td></tr>
<tr><td>

Associating attribute

Poor	Fair	Good	Excellent
1	2	3	4

</td><td>

Evidence from job candidate to back up their rating in this category

</td></tr>
</table>

Observation attributes				Evidence from the job candidate to back up their rating in this category
Poor	Fair	Good	Excellent	
1	2	3	4	

Experimenting attribute				Evidence from the job candidate to back up their rating in this category
Poor	Fair	Good	Excellent	
1	2	3	4	

Envisioning attribute				Evidence from the job candidate to back up their rating in this category
Poor	Fair	Good	Excellent	
1	2	3	4	

Risk taking attributes				Evidence from the job candidate to back up their rating in this category
Poor	Fair	Good	Excellent	
1	2	3	4	

Challenging status quo attribute				Evidence from the job candidate to back up their rating in this category
Poor	Fair	Good	Excellent	
1	2	3	4	

Experiential learning attribute				Evidence from the job candidate to back up their rating in this category
Poor	Fair	Good	Excellent	
1	2	3	4	

Candidates' rating of their overall innovative thinking skills				Evidence from the job candidate to back up their rating based on the definition of innovative thinking skills
Poor	Fair	Good	Excellent	
1	2	3	4	

References: The job candidate should at least list two to three professional references to support their innovative thinking skills and competencies:

Full name:- - - - - - - - - - - - - - - - - Position: - - - - - - - - - - - - - - - - --
Company: - - - - - - - - - - - - - - - - - - - Phone: - - - - - - - - - - - - - - - -
Address: -

Full name:- - - - - - - - - - - - - - - - - Position: - - - - - - - - - - - - - - - - --
Company: - - - - - - - - - - - - - - - - - - - Phone: - - - - - - - - - - - - - - - -
Address: -

Part 2
Determination of Innovation Engagement Skills

As stated earlier, the significance of innovation engagement skills in hiring for innovation is dependent on the leadership roles performed in a job position. This means that innovation engagement skills will be required more in job positions that have a number of leadership roles. Thus, the more leadership roles a job position possesses, the more innovation engagement skills will be required. That being said, there are a number of innovation engagement abilities that can be identified and determined depending on the scale and level of leadership roles in a position.

The purpose of this section is to give opportunity to job candidates to explain how they meet the innovation engagement abilities for the job position. The candidate should be able to give evidence for innovation engagement abilities in a clear and concise manner. Examples of aspects you could look for are outlined below:

Rating scale for innovation engagement skills	Evidence by the job candidate to support their rating

Overall rating of the innovation engagement skills				Job candidates could provide evidence of innovation engagement skills as follows:
Poor	Fair	Good	Excellent	• Examples of abilities to regularly educate and inspire workforces (e.g., at meetings, conferences, or retreats; also brochures, articles, and newsletters) in terms of the vision of the company
1	2	3	4	• Examples of abilities to articulate and communicate various innovation-support initiatives—such as innovation strategies, innovation policies/procedures/plans, innovation goals, and innovation targets—implemented in the organization

Job candidates could provide evidence of innovation engagement skills as follows:

• Examples of abilities to regularly educate and inspire workforces (e.g., at meetings, conferences, or retreats; also brochures, articles, and newsletters) in terms of the vision of the company

• Examples of abilities to articulate and communicate various innovation-support initiatives—such as innovation strategies, innovation policies/procedures/plans, innovation goals, and innovation targets—implemented in the organization

• Examples of abilities to articulate and communicate (in simple and clear terms) the innovation performance of the company in each functional unit or division and in terms of the organization as a whole

• Examples of involvement in educating workforces about various aspects of innovation, such as the meaning of innovation, types of innovation, and the significance of innovation to an organization by giving examples

• Examples of abilities to formulate innovation-motivating slogans, catchphrases, and visual illustrations aimed at contributing toward instilling innovation performance in the hearts and minds of workforces by giving examples

• Examples of abilities to create techniques to effectively communicate innovation-motivating slogans, catchphrases, and visual illustrations aimed at instilling innovation performance in the hearts and minds of workforces by giving examples

• Examples of abilities to exhibit fit-for-purpose attitudes, language, and actions aimed at contributing toward creating an organizational climate that encourages innovative thinking across the organization by giving examples

References: The job candidate should at least list two to three professional references to support their innovative thinking skills and competencies:

Full name:- - - - - - - - - - - - - - - - - - Position: - - - - - - - - - - - - - - - - - --
Company: - - - - - - - - - - - - - - - - - - - Phone: - - - - - - - - - - - - - - - - - -
Address: -
- -
- -
- -

Full name:- - - - - - - - - - - - - - - - - - Position: - - - - - - - - - - - - - - - - - --
Company: - - - - - - - - - - - - - - - - - - - Phone: - - - - - - - - - - - - - - - - - -
Address: -
- -
- -
- -

Part 4
Determination of Innovation Management Skills

Rating scale for innovation management skills	**Evidence by the job candidate to support their rating**
Overall rating of the innovation management skills 	Fair	Good	Excellent
1	2	3	4		Job candidates could provide evidence of innovation engagement skills as follows: • Examples of their abilities to create innovation-performance job duties and responsibilities in their current or previous role • Examples of their abilities to develop and implement product innovation strategies • Examples of their abilities to create product innovation goals in their current or previous functional role • Examples of their abilities to generate innovation-challenge questions for the functional activities of their current or previous role • Examples of their abilities to design and implement a system for management of innovation ideas for product units • Examples of their abilities to structure and report innovation performance in relation to their current or previous role

---

References: The job candidate should at least list two to three professional references to support their innovative thinking skills and competencies:

Full name:- - - - - - - - - - - - - - - - - - Position: - - - - - - - - - - - - - - - -
Company: - - - - - - - - - - - - - - - - - - - Phone: - - - - - - - - - - - - - - - -
Address: -
- -

Full name:- - - - - - - - - - - - - - - - - Position: - - - - - - - - - - - - - - - -
Company: - - - - - - - - - - - - - - - - - - - Phone: - - - - - - - - - - - - - - - -
Address: -
- -

2. Innovation Competencies Selection Process

Once the JAICE forms are received, the next step is the Innovation Competencies Selection Process (I-CS Process). The I-CS Process involves undertaking particular processes and activities to help determine and make decisions on whether or not the job candidate has met the innovation skills and competencies requirements. The following are some of the activities involved in the I-CS Process:

- Innovation competencies selection Committee
- Innovation competencies selection training
- Action plan
- Short-listing job candidates

i. Innovation Competencies Selection Committee

The first step of the I-CS Process is to constitute an Innovation Competencies Selection Committee. The I-CS committee should comprise a diverse team constituted to assess the innovation skills and competencies of job candidates for particular job positions. HR and the head of the user functional unit are supposed to coordinate to determine the composition of the I-CS committee.

ii. **Innovation Competencies Selection Training**

The second step is for HR to arrange the Innovation Competencies Selection Training (I-CS training). This training is aimed at orienting all interviewers that will be involved in the Innovation Competencies Selection Process for a job position. Since each of the I-CS Process is context specific in terms of jobs descriptions and job specifications, the I-CS training should be aligned with the innovation performance requirements of the job under consideration in terms of:

- Innovation skills, abilities, and attributes

- Innovation responsibilities and duties

- Selection interview questioning approaches (i.e. structured and unstructured questioning and which individuals on the panel will ask what question)

- Rating scale and weighted selection evaluation techniques being applied

- General guidelines for conducting the particular innovation competencies selection interview

- Checking references and the worksheets used

The content and delivery methodology of the I-CS training should be planed and implemented by HR and the user department, i.e. the department under which the job position falls.

iii. **Action Plan**

The third step is that once everybody is conversant with the I-CS Process, the I-CS committee should devise an action plan on how the I-CS Process will proceed.

iv. **Short-Listing Job Candidates**

The fourth step is the short-listing of job candidates. As recommended earlier, job candidates should fill out two application forms. That is, the application form for the main technical skills (non-innovation related skills) required to undertake the main duties and responsibilities of the job, and the innovation-related skills and competencies application form (referred here as the Job Applicant Innovation Competencies Elicitation form). The challenge is, how do you deal with the two processes (the non-innovation skills and innovation skills)? We recommend that you regard the main technical skills required to undertake the main duties and responsibilities of the job as the main requirement. In other words, once candidates fulfil the main technical skills and abilities required to undertake the main duties and responsibilities of the job, the next stage is to determine their innovation competencies based on the criticality of innovation in the particular functional unit and innovation performance activities of the job under consideration.

One of the first activities that should be undertaken when conducting the I-CS Process is short-listing the job candidates. What does short listing in the context of innovation competencies mean? In this book, we've defined short-listing candidates in the context of innovation competencies as: *a process of deciding which candidates should be followed up with an innovation competencies selection interview and those that should be immediately ruled out*. Next page is an example of a form that can be used for short-listing candidates who meet essential innovation competencies requirements for a particular job position.

3. **Innovation Competencies Selection Interview**
The innovation competencies selection interview is an opportunity for the selection team to meet the short-listed candidates to probe and inquire about their innovation skills and abilities, attributes, and experience which they have stated in the Job Applicant Innovation Competencies Elicitation Form (the JAICE form). That being said, members of the interview team for any job position should understand that the aim of the

Table 4.4. Example of innovation competencies short-listing form

<table>
<tr><td colspan="4" align="center">Innovation Competencies Short-listing Form

Department: --

Job Position: ---------------------------- Reference: -----------------</td></tr>
<tr><td rowspan="2">Candidate's name</td><td colspan="3">Comments about candidate's innovation skills in terms of suitability</td></tr>
<tr><td>Innovative Thinking Skills</td><td>Innovation Engagement Skills</td><td>Innovation Management Skills</td></tr>
<tr><td></td><td></td><td></td><td></td></tr>
<tr><td></td><td></td><td></td><td></td></tr>
<tr><td></td><td></td><td></td><td></td></tr>
<tr><td></td><td></td><td></td><td></td></tr>
<tr><td></td><td></td><td></td><td></td></tr>
<tr><td colspan="4">Signed:---------------------------------- Date:----------------------------------</td></tr>
</table>

interview is to afford the candidates a chance to show how they qualify or meet the innovation performance competencies outlined in the job. Adequate preparations must be conducted to ensure that the process produces the desired results. Some of the key aspects of the preparations could include: (1) preparing innovation competencies interview questions and (2) creating questions to determine innovation competencies.

i. **Preparing Innovation Competencies Interview Questions**

Questioning is the key aspect of the innovation competencies selection interview process. Like other contexts of employment interview, questioning for innovation competencies selection interview involves generating, creating, and phrasing various structured and unstructured questions that will be used to elicit effective information that will help to come up with accurate decisions on whether or not a job candidate has met the innovation competencies requirements. If the objective of the innovation competencies selection interview questions is to elicit information that will result in making accurate decisions about the job candidates, *what sort of questions do you come up with, and how do you phrase the questions?* Like in any employment interview, *innovation competencies selection panel* must ensure that an appropriate questioning methodology is adopted. In this book, we have suggested the following aspects to bear in mind when creating and phrasing questions.

- *Structured interview questions*: This approach involves creating questions that will be asked to all the candidates, in the same order, without adding additional questions.

- *Unstructured interview questions:* This approach involves asking questions that are not prepared beforehand but instead are asked depending on the responses from interviewees regarding their innovation competencies and experiences. In this approach interviewers can ask immediate questions regarding aspects of any answer that is not clear.

Semi-structured interview questions: This is where some questions are asked to all interviewees, plus some additional questions that the interviewees are asked according to the answers given.

ii. **Creating Questions to Determine Innovation Competencies**

How do you phrase the questions to determine innovation competencies? The questions should be formulated and phrased in such a way that they are effective in eliciting information on which determination of innovation competencies will be based. The JAICE form is a great resource for generating and formulating interview questions. We have divided the JAICE form into the three types of innovation skill sets—namely, innovative thinking skills, innovation engagement skills, and innovation management skills. Each category of innovation skill set has a set of questions formulated to elicit information on which determination of innovation competencies will be based. The table below provides some examples of how to formulate innovation competencies interview questions.

Table 4-5. Example of innovation competencies interview questions form

Innovation Competencies Interview Questions Form
Position:
Name of department:
Date:
Part 1 **Innovative Thinking Skills**
Questions in this category are meant to inquire about the various aspects of the candidate's innovative thinking skills and competencies, in terms of: (1) the ability to identify problems and needs and (2) the ability to turn the problems into innovative opportunities by developing new solutions with potential to contribute monetary value to the organization.

Some innovative thinking skills and competencies to inquire about	Create questions that relate to the innovative thinking attribute or competence under consideration
Questioning attribute	Create and ask interview questions aimed at enabling job candidates to express themselves on how they have used their questioning attribute to generate innovative ideas in their current or previous positions in functional activities relating to how they have rated themselves on this aspect in the JAICE form, i.e. asking them to give examples.
Problem-solving attribute	Create and ask interview questions aimed at enabling job candidates to express themselves on how they have used their problem-solving attribute to generate innovative ideas in their current or previous positions in functional activities relating to how they have rated themselves on this aspect in the JAICE form, i.e. asking them to give examples.
No fear-for-failure attribute	Create and ask interview questions aimed at enabling job candidates to give a description of themselves mirroring the no fear-for-failure attribute and how they used it to generate successful innovative ideas in their current or previous positions in functional activities relating to how they have rated themselves on this aspect in the JAICE form, i.e. asking them to give examples.
Networking attribute	Create and ask interview questions aimed at enabling job candidates to express themselves on how they have used their networking attributes to build and shape their innovative thinking skills. This should include examples of how they intentionally use networking activities as a platform to shape innovative thinking abilities in relation to how they have rated themselves on this aspect in the JAICE form, i.e. asking them to give an example.

Associating attribute	Create and ask interview questions aimed at enabling job candidates to express their ability to practice or engage in interlacing and combining ideas from different areas or fields to solve a particular problem or improve upon the existing solutions, i.e. job candidates should be allowed to give examples of innovative ideas generated from a combination of ideas from different areas or fields.
Observation attributes	Create and ask interview questions aimed at enabling job candidates to express how they have used their observation abilities to identify a need or problem and how they've used it (observing attribute) to generate innovative ideas in the current or previous job, i.e. asking them for examples.
Experimenting attribute	Create and ask interview questions aimed at enabling job candidates to express themselves about their experimenting attributes, i.e. what kind of approaches and techniques do the candidates engage in to practice and enhance their experimenting attributes, i.e. asking them for examples.
Envisioning attribute	Create and ask interview questions aimed at enabling job candidates to express themselves about their ability to understand, predict, or picture key aspects of market (local or global) trends or patterns and whether they've ever leveraged the market patterns or trends to generate or contribute innovative ideas related to how they have rated themselves on this aspect in the JAICE form, i.e. asking them to give examples.
Risk-taking attributes	Create and ask interview questions aimed at enabling job candidates to express themselves about their risk-taking attributes, i.e. asking them to give examples of situations relating to generation and development of innovative ideas that involved risk-taking.

Challenging-status-quo attribute	Create and ask interview questions aimed at enabling job candidates to express themselves about their ability to challenge status quo for improvement purposes relating to how they have rated themselves on this aspect in the JAICE form, i.e. asking them to give examples.
Experiential-learning attribute	Create and ask interview questions aimed at enabling job candidates to express themselves about their ability to learn from past experiences and how they have applied their past experience in the context of ideation, i.e. asking for examples related to how they have rated themselves on this aspect in the JAICE form, i.e. asking them to give examples.

Part 2
Innovation Engagement Skills

As in Part One, the questions in this category are a follow-up to the information provided by the job candidates on the JAICE form. The purpose here is to give candidates the opportunity to express and explain their ratings in relation to the innovation engagement skills and competencies. As stated earlier, the significance of innovation engagement skills in hiring for innovation is dependent upon the leadership roles performed in a job position. If a job position requires innovation engagement skills, job interviewers should create questions aimed enabling job candidates to express their skills and experience for engaging workforces' passion, emotional interest, and commitment to advance innovation across the organization.

Example of interview questions for innovation engagement skills and competencies include the following:

• Create and ask questions aimed at enabling job candidates to express themselves about their ability to regularly educate and inspire workforces about the vision of the company related to how they have rated themselves on this aspect in the JAICE form, i.e. asking for examples.

• Create and ask questions aimed at enabling job candidates to express themselves about their ability to articulate and communicate various innovation-support initiatives—such as innovation strategies, innovation policies/procedures/plans, innovation goals, and innovation targets—implemented in the organization related to how they have rated themselves on this aspect in the JAICE form, i.e. asking for examples.

• Create and ask questions aimed at enabling job candidates to express themselves about their ability to articulate and communicate (in simple and clear terms) the innovation performance of the company related to how they have rated themselves on this aspect in the JAICE form, i.e. asking for examples i.e. ask for examples.

• Create and ask questions aimed at enabling job candidates to express themselves about their ability to educate workforces about various aspects of innovation, such as the meaning of innovation, types of innovation, and the significance of innovation to an organization relatd to how they have rated themselves on this aspect in the JAICE form, i.e. asking for examples.

• Create and ask questions aimed at enabling job candidates to express themselves about their ability to formulate innovation-motivating slogans, catchphrases, and visual illustrations aimed at contributing toward instilling innovation performance in the hearts and minds of workforces related to how they have rated themselves on this aspect in the JAICE form, i.e. asking for examples.

• Create and ask questions aimed at enabling job candidates to express themselves about their ability to exhibit fit-for-purpose attitudes, language, and actions aimed at contributing toward creating an organizational climate that encourages innovative thinking across the organization related to how they have rated themselves on this aspect in the JAICE form, i.e. asking for examples.

Part 3
Innovation Management Skills

This category involves creating and asking interview questions that inquire about various aspects of the candidate's innovation management skills and competencies.

The purpose is to give candidates an opportunity to express and explain their ratings in relation to the innovation management skills and competencies. As stated earlier, the significance of innovation management skills in hiring for innovation is dependent on the leadership roles performed in a job position. If a job position requires innovation management skills, job interviewers should create questions aimed enabling job candidates to express their skills and experience to formulate and implement innovation-support systems. As stated earlier, innovation-support systems are the innovation-support strategies, policies and procedures, structures, etc. aimed at contributing to advancing the culture of innovation across the organization.

Example of interview questions for innovation management skills and competencies include the following:

• Create and ask questions aimed at enabling job candidates to express themselves about their ability to create innovation-performance job duties and responsibilities in their current or previous role in relation to how they have rated themselves on this aspect in the JAICE form, i.e. ask for examples.

• Create and ask questions aimed at enabling job candidates to express themselves about their ability to develop and implement product innovation strategies in relation to how they have rated themselves on this aspect in the JAICE form, i.e. ask for examples.

• Create and ask questions aimed at enabling job candidates to express themselves about their ability to create product innovation goals in their current or previous functional role in relation to how they have rated themselves on this aspect in the JAICE form, i.e. ask for examples.

• Create and ask questions aimed at enabling job candidates to express themselves about their ability to generate innovation-challenge questions for the functional activities of their current or previous role in relation to how they have rated themselves on this aspect in the JAICE form, i.e. ask for examples.

• Create and ask questions aimed at enabling job candidates to express themselves about their ability to design, implement a system for management of innovation ideas for product units in relation to how they have rated themselves on this aspect in the JAICE form, i.e. ask for examples.

• Create and ask questions aimed at enabling job candidates to express themselves about their ability to structure and report innovation performance in relation to their current or previous role in relation to how they have rated themselves on this aspect in the JAICE form, i.e. ask for examples.

Name and position of the interviewer:

iii. **Characteristics of the innovation competencies interview questions**

Earlier we asked a question that if the objective of the innovation competencies selection interview questions is to elicit information that will result in making accurate decisions about the job candidates, i.e. *what sort of questions then do you come up with and how do you phrase the questions?* In addition to the aspects that have been indicated above regarding how to generate and create questions for the JAICE form, here are some general characteristics of innovation competencies interview questions:

- Create a format for who asks which questions.
- Arrange for one person to be specifically taking notes without taking part in asking questions.
- Each question should be relevant to the particular innovation skill/competencies that you are looking for. In other words, the question must be related to the innovation job description elements and person specification.
- Ask questions that bring out information from candidates that can easily be aligned to the weighting mechanism and the rating scales.
- The questions must be focused and clear so that the candidate is not lost.
- All structured questions must be repeated to all the candidates the same way.

- Ask the questions in the logical order according to the category of questions you have come up with.
- Create questions that allow candidates to do most of the talking.
- Come up with follow up questions or probe more deeply with further questions if you think the candidate needs to expand on an answer.

Other Aspects of Characteristics of the Innovation Competencies Interview Questions Include *Open-ended* and *Closed* Questions

i. *Open-ended questions:* These are questions that require more than just "*Yes*" or "*No*" answers. Like in other types of job interviews, innovation competencies interviews require probing (make sure to use a tone that is not intimidating) so that you are able elicit the required information. Open-ended questions allow candidates to do most of the talking. Below are some examples of open-ended questions:

- Can you tell us what you know about our company's innovation policy and practices?
- Can you tell us what you understand about innovation strategy?
- Can you tell us what you understand about *radical* and *incremental* innovation?
- Can you tell us how you came up with your last 2 product innovation ideas and production process innovation ideas?

- Can you briefly outline some of the approaches that you have developed and implemented to champion innovation in your current or previous company, and what impact did the approaches have?

ii. *Closed questions:* On the other hand, closed questions are questions that require just "*Yes*" or "*No*" answers without further outline or explanation. Some examples of closed questions are:

- Do you know anything about some of our company innovation policies and practices?

- Have you ever taken part in designing any kind of innovation strategy?

- Have you ever generated a product or service innovation idea that was further developed and eventually launched on the market?

- Have you ever been involved in a team generated product or service innovation idea that was further developed and eventually launched on the market?

- How many patents do you have?

- When was your last patent obtained?

- Have you ever managed an innovation project from conception through development to market launch?

- Have you ever written an innovation performance report?

4. **Candidates' Innovation Competencies Assessment**
One of the critical elements in the innovation competencies interview selection process is the Candidates' Innovation Competencies Assessment form (CICA form). The CICA form can be used for recording innovation competencies assessment of each candidate during the interview. How do you create the CICA form? What constitutes CICA form? In non-innovation-related competencies interview selection assessment process, creating candidate assessment models varies from organization to organization. Similarly, creating innovation competencies interview selection assessment methods varies from organization to organization. Based on this, HR and the head of the functional unit under which the position being considered falls should lead the panel to create an appropriate CICA form.

The CICA form suggested involves selecting and listing desired *innovation skills, competencies* and *attributes* that are outlined in the job description and job specification of the position under consideration. The major element of the CICA form is the weighting and rating scale which play a critical role in selecting a candidate with the right innovation skills and competencies in relation to the job position.

The CICA form should be completed by members of the interview panel during each interview, and the ratings assigned by each interviewer will form the basis for the discussion at the end of the interviews and will be used to make the final selection decision.

The following are some of the contents of the CICA form:

- Each category of innovation skills is differentially weighted according to its importance to the functional unit and job position under consideration.
- Assign a weighting according to how important each category of innovation skill / competence is to the job position under consideration.
- After each interview, rate the candidate for each category of innovation skill / competence or attribute on a rating scale. Here is an example of a rating scale:
  - 1=Poor
  - 2=Fair
  - 3=Good
  - 4=Excellent
- Final calculations of the score for each candidate: Multiply the weighting for each category of innovation skill/competence or attribute by the performance rating allocated to the candidate in each category of innovation skills.
- Sum up all the multiplied ratings to obtain a total.
- Then rank the innovation competencies of the candidates according to their total scores.

The above can be illustrated in the CICA form as follows:

Table 4-6. Example innovation competencies assessment form

Position:--

Department:------------------------------

Position Reference:-----------------------------------

Name of the interviewer: ----------------------------------

Date:--

Innovation skills, competencies & attributes	Weights	*Candidate A*		*Candidate B*		*Candidate C*	
		Rating	Score	Rating	Score	Rating	Score
Innovative thinking skills: List critical innovative thinking competencies desired for this position.	40						
Innovation engagement skills: List critical innovation engagement skills and abilities desired for this position.	20						
Innovation management skills: List critical innovative thinking competencies desired for this position.	30						

Other innovation attributes: List innovative attributes that are critical or desired for this position.	10					
Total scores						
Interviewer's signature:---						

Key Aspects

- Ensure that the desired competencies that you outline in the CICA form are simple and easily identifiable and distinguishable in candidates and that the assigned rating should reflect the candidate's strength in each category of innovation skills and competencies.

- Also, scoring must show a clear choice of candidate, but if there is no clear choice, further discussion may be required and the justification for the final choice must be recorded. To help determine a clear choice of candidate, you could ask questions such as:

  - Do the scores reflect a clear choice of candidate? **Yes/No**

  - If **No**, what factors lead to the choice of candidate?

5. **Post- Innovation Competencies Selection Interview**

   Once you are done with the innovation selection assessment, the next stage is to apply your organization's after-interview procedures which usually include the following:

- Checking references

- Offer of employment to successful candidate

- Reserve candidates

- Notification of unsuccessful candidates

- Induction

- Probationary period

- Probationary period reviews

- Decision making at the end of probationary period

6. **Reconciling Technical and Innovation Competencies to Make a Selection**

At the beginning of this chapter, we emphasized that the process of identifying innovation competencies in job candidates should be conducted as a separate process from the selection process that focuses on identifying main technical competencies of the job candidates. Based on this, job candidates should fill out two application forms: *the technical competencies-centered application form* and the *Job Applicant Innovation Competencies Elicitation Form* (JAICE form). This section focuses on reconciling the two dimensions of skill sets—the technical competencies and innovation competencies to make a decision on which candidates meet the requirements for the job.

You could be confronted with a scenario where candidates fail to score high interview ratings in innovation competencies but perform well in the technical requirements of the job—or just the opposite.

For instance, if you are selecting a candidate for the position of a *Marketing Manager* and you have 3 candidates (X, Y and Z) undergoing a selection process, think of how you would treat a situation where:

- Candidate "X" scores *high* in non-innovation competencies but records *low* scores in innovation competencies
- Or candidate "Y" scores *higher* in innovation competencies than "X", but *lower* in technical competencies (non-innovation competencies)
- Candidate "Z" also scores higher in one but extremely lower in the other

To avoid the above scenario, the leadership should ensure that likely scenarios of selection challenges are worked out well in advance and that suggestions on how to deal with them are brainstormed and adopted as recruitment measures.

The following are some ways to deal with the above scenario:

- State clearly the aspects of competencies that are critical to the position that you are seeking candidates for. In other words, is it the technical skill sets (*non-innovation competencies*) that are critical to the position or innovation competencies? This will help you choose a candidate who meets the critical competencies.

- Ensure that the job advert describes in simple and concise terms the critical (*must-have*) activities and requirements of the job. This will encourage only individuals that meet the set requirements to apply for the position.
- Ensure that you use effective techniques for eliciting evidence of competencies from job candidates.
- You could also consider re-advertising the position.

Chapter Five

IDENTIFYING INNOVATIVE THINKING POTENTIAL FOR ENTRY LEVEL JOBS

Overview

Up until this point, the discussion in this book has focused on tools, steps, and mechanisms for identifying the three categories of innovation skill sets or competencies in individuals seeking job opportunities in *experienced positions*. This chapter focuses on tools and approaches for identifying innovative thinking potential in individuals seeking job opportunities in entry-level positions.

We define entry level position as an organization's job positions whose requirements are fulfilled by individuals who have just finished college or university or individuals who may have worked elsewhere but wish to join the organization as *entry associates*. What this means is that the approaches for hiring for innovation in experienced job positions and entry-level positions are different. For instance, while experienced hires such as an assistant or a senior manager in a particular functional unit may be required to possess, to a certain degree, all the three types of innovation skills, it is not necessary for job candidates seeking entry positions to have all the three types of innovation skill sets. So, what types of innovation skills are necessary for entry positions? This chapter focuses on this question.

Step 13: Identifying Innovative Thinking Potential for Entry Level Jobs

In this final step, (chapter five), we look at the correct category of innovation skills to look for in first time entrants (i.e. college or university graduates) or job candidates seeking job opportunities in entry or associate level positions. Recall that the value of contribution to innovation performance by workforces depends on the level and type of innovation skill set that they possess and how the innovation abilities are applied. We further stated that for hiring managers to hire job candidates with the level and type of innovation skill sets that will contribute meaningful innovation performance to the functional unit, it is important for hiring managers to understand the different contexts of innovation skill sets that are being sought in job candidates. For instance, the categories of innovation skill sets required for experienced hires is different from first time entrants or associate level positions.

When interviewing and assessing job candidates for positions that require experience and leadership roles, all the three types or categories of innovation skill sets should be considered—namely innovative thinking skills, innovation engagement skills, and innovation management skills. However, based on the context of what each of the types of innovation skill sets entail, not all three innovation skill sets would be required in job positions for first time entrants (i.e. college or university graduates) or associate level positions. Based on the context of what each of the types of innovation skill sets entail and the roles that are usually performed in associate level positions, the ideal type of innovation skill set needed is innovative thinking skills.

Definition of Innovative Thinking Potential

Remember, when discussing innovative thinking skills for experienced hires in chapter four, we said that there are three aspects involved when determining innovative thinking skills in experienced hires. Similarly, the three aspects should be identified in the following context:

- First, *potential and ability to identify problems:* This involves the ability of the job candidates to identify problems, needs, and challenges in the context of the organization's business model and the context of the functional activities and the job position. Remember, innovative thinking skills can be expressed and applied across industries—financial, insurance, health, hospitality, media, entertainment, food, telecommunications, and manufacturing. However, in first time entrants, such as college graduates and individuals with a bit of experience but seeking associate level positions, their exposure to the corporate world is very limited to none. So, in order to determine the ability or potential to identify problems in first time entrants, life-experience context or perspective should be applied. That is, you should be looking at the candidates' ability to identify problems, needs, and challenges in the context of their past life experiences and activities and how they will be able to translate their past life experiences and academic activities into the job activities they are applying for.

- Second, *potential and ability to turn problems into innovation opportunities:* This involves determining the potential for the job candidates to turn the needs and the problems into creative ideas by *generating new ideas* or solutions to fix the identified problem or need. Information about the potential of the job candidates can be obtained by formulating and asking questions aimed at eliciting responses that are easily interpreted to determine whether the candidate possesses the idea-generation potential to contribute to the culture of innovation that the organization is pursuing.

- Third, *potential innovative attributes:* Recall when determining innovative attributes in experienced job candidates, we defined innovative attributes as: *character traits or personal qualities that an innovative thinking person can attain and possess and help them drive their innovative performance in a variety of contexts*. This definition can also be applied to first time entrants or associate positions. However, when it comes to harnessing the innovative attributes to identify and assess job candidates who have potential for innovative thinking skills, the questions should be phrased in a manner that would elicit information that suggest potential for innovative thinking skills or lack thereof. The following is a list of examples of how to harness innovative attributes to identify job candidates with potential for innovative thinking skills.

○ **Questioning attribute:** Formulate questions that will help job candidates to reveal whether they possess the questioning attribute, i.e. whether the job candidate has the attributes that constantly question the *what, why* and *how* about something. Let them express themselves on how they have used this attribute in any projects and activities. Formulate questions to elicit information on how job candidates have harnessed their questioning attributes to find alternative ways to solve problems.

○ **Problem-solving attributes:** Formulate questions to elicit information on how job candidates have used their problem-solving attributes to generate ideas in projects and activities that they have been involved in.

- **No fear-for-failure attributes:** Formulate questions aimed at eliciting information from job candidates about how they perceive failure in relation to their life experiences.

- **Networking attributes:** Formulate questions aimed at eliciting information from job candidates about their networking activities and how they have used such activities to help develop their critical and creative or innovative thinking abilities.

- **Associating attributes:** Formulate questions aimed at eliciting information from job candidates that reveals a pattern of behaviour that involves constant practice of engaging in interlacing and combining ideas from different areas or fields to solve a particular problem or improve something.

- **Observing attributes:** Formulate questions aimed at eliciting information from job candidates about their observation abilities, how they have used the observation abilities to identify a need or problem, and how they've used it (observing attribute) to generate an innovative idea.

- **Experimenting attributes:** Formulate questions aimed at eliciting information from job candidates about their experimenting attributes, i.e. what kinds of approaches and techniques do the candidate engage in to practice enhancing their experimenting attributes.

- **Risk-taking attributes:** Formulate questions aimed at eliciting information from job candidates about their risking-taking attributes and how they've applied the attributes in their life experiences.

- **Challenging status quo attributes:** Formulate questions aimed at eliciting information from job candidates about whether they possess the attribute for challenging status quo for improvement purposes.

- **Experiential-learning attribute:** Formulate questions aimed at eliciting information from job candidates about the attribute of learning from past experiences and how they have applied their past experiences to generate ideas of any kind.

- **Novel ideas for college projects:** Formulate questions aimed at eliciting information from job candidates about any projects that they undertook in college. Inquire about how many of those new idea projects were successful, and the candidate should define success in the context of the projects.

- **Grit attributes:** To compete in today's rapidly changing and highly competitive world, companies must look beyond traditional performance attributes when hiring talent for innovation. One such attribute is grit. According to the Merriam Webster dictionary, grit is: *the firmness of mind or spirit or unyielding courage in the face of hardship.* That being said, formulate questions aimed at eliciting information from job candidates about any stories or life experiences that reflect firmness of mind.

Mechanisms for Identifying Innovative Thinking Potential

In chapter four we discussed mechanisms for rating the criticality of innovation skills and how to identify the right innovation skills in job candidates seeking experienced positions. In this section, as said before, we look at mechanisms for rating and identifying the right innovation skills in job candidates seeking entry positions. We begin with innovative thinking skills and what selection mechanisms you apply to identify potential innovative thinking skills in first time entrants. There are a number of tools suggested in this book.

1. **Rating Scale**

   The starting point, as said before, is to understand that every employee has the potential to contribute to innovation performance in the context of functional activities of the organization. Based on this, the question that the leadership of the organization would then pose is whether or not innovation is perceived as everybody's responsibility in the organization. If the answer is yes, then two types of rating scales on how critical innovative thinking skills are would be created as follows: (i) criticality of innovative ideas in the functional unit and (ii) criticality of innovative thinking skills in the job position.

Table 5-1. Criticality of innovative thinking ideas in the functional unit

Department:--------------------------------				
	Not critical	Slightly Critical	Moderately Critical	Very Critical	Extremely Critical
Criticality of innovative thinking ideas in the functional unit	1	2	3	4	5
	Indicate the rating in the box below and reasons for the choice of the rating				

Table 5-2. Criticality of innovative thinking skills in the position

Department:--------------------------------				
	Not critical	Slightly Critical	Moderately Critical	Very Critical	Extremely Critical
Criticality of innovative thinking skills in the position under consideration	1	2	3	4	5
	Indicate the rating in the box below, and reasons for the choice of the rating				

2. **Identifying Innovative Thinking Potential in Job Candidates**

The following are some of the steps and tools for identifying and determining innovative thinking potential in job candidates seeking job opportunities in entry or associate level positions

i. **Training for Selecting Innovative Thinking Potential**

Similar to the selection process for position roles requiring experienced candidates discussed in *step 12*, managers or teams responsible for hiring individuals seeking associate positions should be trained in the selection process for identifying innovative thinking potential in job candidates. The interviewers should be oriented through all the general guidelines for identifying the right candidates. Guidelines comprise selection procedures and tools for determining innovative thinking potential such as:

- Innovative thinking attributes considered as critical that are being sought after in job candidates
- Innovative thinking-related responsibilities and duties that job candidates are expected to fulfil
- Selection interview questioning approaches (i.e. structured and unstructured questioning in which individuals on the hiring panel will ask)
- Rating scale and weighted selection evaluation techniques for determining innovative potential

ii. **Job Applicant Innovative Thinking Potential Elicitation Form (JAITPE form):** Similar to the JAICE described in chapter four, *step 12*, the JAITPE form is used to elicit information from job candidates seeking job opportunities in entry or associate level positions about their innovative thinking potential. Again, similar to *step 12*, the JAITPE form should be administered to job candidates as a supplementary process after determining the technical or core job-related requirements of the position. The same committee or task force established to create the JAICE form, *step 12*, should create the JAITPE form. The following is an example of the JAITPE form:

Table 5-3. Example of job applicant innovative thinking potential elicitation form

Job Applicant Innovative Thinking Potential Elicitation Form (JAITPE Form)
Name of job applicant:
Position title being applied for:
Name of department:
Date on which form was filled:
Phone #:
E-mail:

<table>
<tr><td colspan="2">Determining Innovative Thinking Potential</td></tr>
<tr><td colspan="2">Interpretation: State the meaning of innovative thinking potential as defined by the organization. For instance, you could interpret it as the possession of identifiable innovation thinking attributes in job candidates seeking first time entrants in the world of work or job candidates seeking job opportunities in entry or associate level positions.

Rating scale: Job candidates rate themselves against the innovative thinking skills and attributes outlined below.</td></tr>
<tr><td>Rating scale for innovative thinking potential</td><td>Evidence by job candidate to support their rating choice</td></tr>
<tr><td>Questioning attribute

<table><tr><td>Poor</td><td>Fair</td><td>Good</td><td>Excellent</td></tr><tr><td>1</td><td>2</td><td>3</td><td>4</td></tr></table></td><td>Evidence from the job candidate to back up their rating based on the definition of innovative thinking potential</td></tr>
<tr><td>Problem-solving attribute

<table><tr><td>Poor</td><td>Fair</td><td>Good</td><td>Excellent</td></tr><tr><td>1</td><td>2</td><td>3</td><td>4</td></tr></table></td><td>Evidence from the job candidate to back up their rating based on the definition of innovative thinking potential</td></tr>
<tr><td>No fear-for-failure attribute

<table><tr><td>Poor</td><td>Fair</td><td>Good</td><td>Excellent</td></tr><tr><td>1</td><td>2</td><td>3</td><td>4</td></tr></table></td><td>Evidence from the job candidate to back up their rating based on the definition of innovative thinking potential</td></tr>
<tr><td>Networking attribute

<table><tr><td>Poor</td><td>Fair</td><td>Good</td><td>Excellent</td></tr><tr><td>1</td><td>2</td><td>3</td><td>4</td></tr></table></td><td>Evidence from the job candidate to back up their rating based on the definition of innovative thinking potential</td></tr>
</table>

Associating attribute				Evidence from the job candidate to back up their rating based on the definition of innovative thinking potential
Poor	Fair	Good	Excellent	
1	2	3	4	

Observing attributes				Evidence from the job candidate to back up their rating based on the definition of innovative thinking potential
Poor	Fair	Good	Excellent	
1	2	3	4	

Experimenting attribute				Evidence from the job candidate to back up their rating based on the definition of innovative thinking potential
Poor	Fair	Good	Excellent	
1	2	3	4	

Envisioning attribute				Evidence from the job candidate to back up their rating based on the definition of innovative thinking potential
Poor	Fair	Good	Excellent	
1	2	3	4	

Risk-taking attributes				Evidence from the job candidate to back up their rating based on the definition of innovative thinking potential
Poor	Fair	Good	Excellent	
1	2	3	4	

Challenging-status-quo attribute				Evidence from the job candidate to back up their rating based on the definition of innovative thinking potential
Poor	Fair	Good	Excellent	
1	2	3	4	

Experiential-attribute				Evidence from the job candidate to back up their rating based on the definition of innovative thinking potential
Poor	Fair	Good	Excellent	
1	2	3	4	

Grit attributes				Evidence from the job candidate to back up their rating based on the definition of innovative thinking potential
Poor	Fair	Good	Excellent	
1	2	3	4	

Novel ideas for college projects				Evidence from the job candidate to back up their rating based on the definition of innovative thinking potential
Poor	Fair	Good	Excellent	
1	2	3	4	

References: The job candidate could obtain at least one to two references to support their innovative thinking potential.

Full name:- Position: - - - - - - - - - - - - - - - - - -

Company: - - - - - - - - - - - - - - - - - - - Phone: - - - - - - - - - - - - - - - - -

Address: -

Full name:- Position: - - - - - - - - - - - - - - - - - -

Company: - - - - - - - - - - - - - - - - - - - Phone: - - - - - - - - - - - - - - - - -

Address: -

iii. **Short-Listing Job Candidates**

Again, as discussed in step 12 about the short-listing of job candidates for experienced positions, job candidates should fill out two application forms—the application form for the main technical skills (non-innovative-related thinking) required to undertake the main duties and responsibilities of the job and the innovative-related thinking potential, referred to as the JAITPE form. Once candidates fulfill the main technical skills and abilities required to undertake the main duties and responsibilities of the job, the next stage is to determine their innovative thinking potential based on the criticality of innovation in the particular functional unit and innovative thinking abilities required in the job under consideration.

Short-listing candidates in the context of their innovative thinking potential is *a process that involves deciding which candidates should be followed up with for an innovative thinking potential selection interview and those that should be immediately ruled out*. Again, the short-listing will be guided by the criticality of innovation in the particular functional unit and innovative thinking abilities required in the job under consideration. So, if some job candidates have met the main technical skills (non-innovative-related thinking) required to undertake the main duties and responsibilities of the job and fall short on innovative thinking potential, a decision has to be made based on the criticality of innovation in the function unit and innovative thinking required in the job under consideration.

Here is an example of a form for short-listing job candidates who meet required levels of innovative thinking potential for a job position.

Table 5-4. Example of innovative thinking potential short-listing form

Innovative Thinking Potential Short-listing Form	
Department: --------------------------------- Job Position:--------------------------------- Reference:----------------	
Candidate's name	Comments about candidate's innovative thinking potential

Signed:---

Date:---

iv. **Selection Interview for Innovative Thinking Potential**

Similar to the innovation competencies selection interview process for experienced hires which we discussed in *step 12*, the selection interview for innovative thinking potential is an opportunity for the selection team or hiring manager to meet the short-listed candidates to probe and inquire about their innovative thinking potential which they have stated in the JAITPE form. So, the aim of the interview is to afford the job candidates a chance to show how they qualify or meet the innovative thinking potential requirements outlined in the job. Again, adequate preparations must be undertaken to ensure that the process produces the desired results—in this case, identifying job candidates that meet innovative thinking requirements of the job position. Similar to conducting the innovation competencies selection interview process, the following two aspects are important when preparing for selection interview for innovative thinking potential: (1) prepare innovative thinking potential-interview questions and (2) create questions to determine innovative thinking potential.

As in innovation competencies selection interview process in *step 12*, questioning for innovative thinking potential involves generating, creating, and phrasing various structured and unstructured questions that will be used to elicit effective information that will help to come up with accurate decisions on whether or not a job candidate has the required level of innovative thinking potential needed for the job position. The questioning methodology for eliciting information that will result in making accurate decisions about the job candidates with the right innovative thinking potential is the same as the one adopted for experienced hires; in step 12 is three dimensions of questioning. Namely, structured interview questions, unstructured interview questions, and semi-structured interview questions.

v. **Create Questions to Determine Innovative Thinking Potential**

How do you phrase the questions to determine innovative thinking potential? Again, as in innovation competencies selection interview process for the experienced hired which we discussed in *step 12*, the questions should be formulated and phrased in a way that they are effective in eliciting information on which determination of innovative thinking potential will be based. The JAITPE form is a great resource for generating and formulating interview questions. The form could be used to formulate and phrase the interview questions for eliciting data about the job candidate's innovative thinking potential data. Here is an example of a simple form for stating innovative thinking potential interview questions.

Table 5-5. Example of innovative thinking potential interview questions form

Innovative Thinking Potential Interview Questions Form	
Position:	
Name of department:	
Date:	
The innovative thinking potential-interview questions are meant to inquire about the various aspects of the candidate's innovative thinking potential. This is done by asking questions that relate to each of the innovative thinking attributes listed in this form. The questions should be aimed at enabling job candidates to state and connect their answers during the interview to the information they provided in the JAITPE form.	
List of innovative thinking attributes to inquire about	**Create questions that relate to the innovative thinking attribute**
Questioning attribute	Create and ask interview questions aimed at enabling job candidates to express their questioning attribute by relating their answers to the rating and information they provided in the JAITPE form, i.e. ask for examples relating to the questioning attribute.
Problem-solving attribute	Create and ask interview questions aimed at enabling job candidates to express their problem-solving attribute by relating their answers to the rating and information they provided in the JAITPE form ,i.e. ask for examples relating to the problem-solving attribute.
No fear-for-failure attribute	Create and ask interview questions aimed at enabling job candidates to express their no fear-for-failure attribute by relating their answers to the rating and information they provided in the JAITPE form, i.e. ask for examples relating to the no fear-for-failure attribute.

Networking attribute	Create and ask interview questions aimed at enabling job candidates to express their networking attribute by relating their answers to the rating and information they provided in the JAITPE form, i.e. ask for examples relating to the networking attribute.
Associating attribute	Create and ask interview questions aimed at enabling job candidates to express their associating attribute by relating their answers to the rating and information they provided in the JAITPE form, i.e. ask for examples relating to the associating attribute.
Observing attributes	Create and ask interview questions aimed at enabling job candidates to express their observing attribute by relating their answers to the rating and information they provided in the JAITPE form, i.e. ask for examples relating to the observing attribute.
Experimenting attribute	Create and ask interview questions aimed at enabling job candidates to express their experimenting attribute by relating their answers to the rating and information they provided in the JAITPE form, i.e. ask for examples relating to the experimenting attribute.
Envisioning attribute	Create and ask interview questions aimed at enabling job candidates to express their envisioning attribute by relating their answers to the rating and information they provided in the JAITPE form, i.e. ask for examples relating to the envisioning attribute.
Risk-taking attributes	Create and ask interview questions aimed at enabling job candidates to express their risking taking attribute by relating their answers to the rating and information they provided in the JAITPE form, i.e. ask for examples relating to the risk taking attribute.
Challenging-status-quo attribute	Create and ask interview questions aimed at enabling job candidates to express their challenging-status-quo attribute by relating their answers to the rating and information they provided in the JAITPE form, i.e. ask for examples relating to the challenging-status-quo attribute.

Experiential-learning attribute	Create and ask interview questions aimed at enabling job candidates to express their experiential-learning attribute by relating their answers to the rating and information they provided in the JAITPE form, i.e. ask for examples relating to the experiential-learning attribute.
Grit attributes	Create and ask interview questions aimed at enabling job candidates to express their grit attribute by relating their answers to the rating and information they provided in the JAITPE form, i.e. ask for examples relating to the grit attribute.

vi. Rating Innovative Thinking Potential of Job Candidates

Remember in *step 12* we gave an example of a tool called CICA for assessing innovation competencies of experienced hires during the interview. We also outlined steps to apply the tool. When interviewing job candidates seeking job opportunities in entry positions, we used a tool that is slightly different from CICA, the Innovative Thinking-Potential Rating Scale (I-TPRS). Similar to CICA, the I-TPRS should be completed by the interviewers during each interview, and the ratings assigned by each interviewer will form basis of the discussion at the end of the interviews. It will be used to make the final selection decision of the job candidate(s) with the required level of innovative thinking potential.

The following are simple steps for administering the I-TPRS.

- Create a list of innovative thinking attributes
- Each category of innovative thinking attributes is differentially weighted according to its importance to the functional unit and job position under consideration.
- Assign a weighting according to how important each innovative thinking attribute is to the open job position
- During the interview, each interviewer assigns a score against each weighted attribute proportionate to the interviewer's perception of how the candidate has outlined and articulated possession of each listed attribute
- Add the overall total score obtained by each candidate: Each interviewer sum up all scores he/she has allocated to each attribute
- Relate the total scores of each candidate to the rating scale
- Then rank the job candidates according to their rating performance

Example

Assume a hiring team of an insurance company is interviewing candidates to fill five entry-level job positions of data analysts. The following would be an example of the innovative thinking potential rating procedure.

Table 5-6. Example of innovative thinking potential rating

<table>
<tr><td colspan="3" align="center">Innovative Thinking Potential Rating</td></tr>
<tr><td colspan="3">Department:------------------------------------</td></tr>
<tr><td colspan="3">Position: Data Analyst</td></tr>
<tr><td colspan="3">Name of Interviewee: Ben Ozil</td></tr>
<tr><td colspan="3">Criticality of innovative thinking in the user department: 4</td></tr>
<tr><td colspan="3">Position Reference:--</td></tr>
<tr><td colspan="3">Name of the Interviewer: Pete Diaby   Position: Senior Manager</td></tr>
<tr><td colspan="3">Date: February 12, 2019</td></tr>
<tr><td>Innovative thinking attribute</td><td>Weights</td><td>Score obtained per attribute by the candidate</td></tr>
<tr><td>Questioning attribute</td><td>40</td><td></td></tr>
<tr><td>Problem-solving attribute</td><td>40</td><td></td></tr>
<tr><td>Challenging-status quo attribute</td><td>35</td><td></td></tr>
<tr><td>Experimenting attribute</td><td>30</td><td></td></tr>
<tr><td>Experiential-learning attribute</td><td>25</td><td></td></tr>
<tr><td>No fear-for-failure attribute</td><td>20</td><td></td></tr>
<tr><td>Networking attribute</td><td>20</td><td></td></tr>
<tr><td>Associating attribute</td><td>15</td><td></td></tr>
<tr><td>Observing attribute</td><td>15</td><td></td></tr>
<tr><td>Envisioning attribute</td><td>10</td><td></td></tr>
<tr><td>Risk-taking attribute</td><td>10</td><td></td></tr>
<tr><td>Total weighting</td><td>260</td><td>Total score obtained:</td></tr>
</table>

> **Average score by the job candidate:** If there is more than one interviewer, an average score should be obtained from each interviewer, calculate the average, and then subject the *average* score of the candidate to the rating scale below.
>
> | Innovative Thinking Potential Rating Scale | |
> | --- | --- |
> | **Level of innovative thinking potential** | **Corresponding range of ratings for each level of innovative thinking potential** |
> | Low or no innovative thinking potential | 0-50 |
> | Average innovative thinking potential | 51-100 |
> | Moderate innovative thinking potential | 101-150 |
> | High innovative thinking potential | 151-220 |
> | Exceptional innovative thinking potential | 221-260 |
>
> **Decision:** *Based on the range of ratings gained by the job candidate under consideration, what is the overall level of innovative thinking potential of the candidate? Is it low, average, moderate high or exceptional?*
>
> **Interviewer's signature:**

3. Post-Selection Interview

In *step 12* of chapter four, we provided a list of aspects to undertake in the aftermath of the innovation competencies selection interview. The same aspects would be applied to the selection interview for innovative thinking potential.

4. **Reconciling Technical Competencies and Innovative Thinking Potential**

    Similarly, when it comes to the aspect of reconciling technical competencies and innovative thinking potential of the job candidates at entry level, the same principle used in identifying innovation competencies in experienced hires, discussed in step 12 of chapter 12, would be applied here.

Create Guidelines for Innovation Talent Recruitment

We end this book with a recommendation of important aspects to outline regarding adoption of the culture of hiring for innovation.

In order to ensure maximum leverage of the innovation talent recruitment process and help institutionalize the practice of hiring for innovation, it's important that the leadership of the organization creates a brochure that outlines two key elements: the organization's policy on hiring for innovation and second, procedures that clearly outline implementation details of the organization's innovation talent recruitment policy.

Generally, the innovation talent recruitment policy guidelines should outline the following elements:

i. In line with the organization's business model and functional units, describe the background and intent that have led to the adoption of innovation talent recruitment practices.

ii. Description of procedures indicating how the innovation talent recruitment policy shall be implemented.

iii. The procedures should indicate, clearly, which parties in the organization are responsible for carrying out actions in relation to the innovation talent recruitment policy.

iv. Guidelines should clearly indicate:
- when the innovation talent recruitment policy comes into effect,
- when and how the policy and its procedures shall be reviewed, and
- parties responsible for the review

Summary

Let's recap the five main aspects the book has covered:

i. Study after study shows that though innovation is a top priority in most industries across the globe, corporations are experiencing difficulties in finding job candidates with the right innovation skills to advance innovation.

ii. Innovation talent recruitment practices are an essential component for building corporate innovation capabilities, which is a vital capability for advancing corporate-wide innovation performance.

iii. Because of the critical role that innovation talent plays in advancing innovation across functional units, it is vital for organizations to enact recruitment strategies for hiring innovation talent if organizations are to advance innovation performance across functional units.

iv. Structured in thirteen steps, the book is segmented in five chapters for designing and implementing a mechanism or framework of tools for identifying innovation skills in job candidates.

v. Tools for identifying, assessing, and determining the right innovation skills and other innovation attributes in job candidates for both experienced and entry level hires.

SELECTED NOTES

Aon 2014 Survey, https://www.aonhewitt.com.au/Home/
Resources/Reports-and-research/2014-Trends-in-Global-
Employee-Engagement

Annual International Conference on Development and Open Innovation Report, 2013

Boston Consulting Group's survey of 2015 Most Innovative
Companies https://www.rankingthebrands.com/PDF/The%20
Most%20Innovative%20Companies%202015,%20Boston%20
Consulting%20Group.pdf

Chartered Institute of Professional and Development (CIPD)/ Hays
2015 Resourcing and Talent Planning Survey https://www.
cipd.co.uk/Images/resourcing-talent-planning_2015_tcm18-
11303.pdf

Global KPMG, Survey 2014, https://home.kpmg/content/dam/
kpmg/pdf/2014/07/war-for-talent.pdf

Hay Group Report, 2015 www.oracle.com/us/products/applica-
tions/oracle-hcm-cloud-2961508.pdf
https://www2.deloitte.com/content/dam/Deloitte/global/Docu-
ments/About-Deloitte/gx-dttl-2014-millennial-survey-report.
pdf

Impact of Tech Talent Shortage: http://blog.indeed.
com/2016/12/05/impact-of-tech-talent-shortage/
Manpower Group Report Manpower Group Report, 2015
https://www.worldgovernmentsummit.org/api/publications/
document?id=a76994c4-e97c-6578-b2f8-ff0000a7ddb6
PwC 2017 CEO20 Survey, https://www.pwc.com/us/en/library/
ceo-agenda/ceo-survey.html

www.ingramcontent.com/pod-product-compliance
Lightning Source LLC
Chambersburg PA
CBHW051456050726
47593CB00005B/2096